ELECTRA IN A ONE-PIECE

Isaac Oliver

I0139647

BROADWAY PLAY PUBLISHING INC
New York
www.broadwayplaypublishing.com
info@broadwayplaypublishing.com

ELECTRA IN A ONE-PIECE
© Copyright 2013 by Isaac Oliver

Cover art by Gabriel Aronson
First printing: December 2013
I S B N: 978-0-88145-578-6
Book design: Marie Donovan
Typographic controls: Adobe Indesign
Typeface: Palatino
Printed and bound in the U S A

ELECTRA IN A ONE-PIECE was first produced by
Wild Project in New York, running from 29 October-14
November 2010. The cast and creative contributors
were:

ORE .... Chris Bannow
BUDDY COX/NON ....Michael Brusasco
ELLE .... Amanda Scot Ellis
FEMALE CHORUS..................................... Melanie Hopkins
LAD ....Ian McWethy
THUS .... Austin Mitchell
MALE CHORUS.. Matt Park
CLYT..Erika Rolfsrud

Director... David Ruttura
Set design ....Kenneth Grady Barker
Costume design .... Moria Sine Clinton
Lighting design ....Paul Toben
Lighting design ....Jeremy Cunningham
Original music ....Ryan Scott Oliver
Sound design.. Jason Crystal
Projection design...Dustin O'Neill
Fight direction... Rick Sordelet
Production stage manager .... Allison Deutsch

CHARACTERS & SETTING

ELLE, *age 16*

CLYT, *("Klight"), age 44*

ORE, *("Orr"), age 18*

LAD, *age 19*

THUS, *([hard first syllable] "Th/us"), age 18*

ETHEL, *age 46*
DR EDITH HAMILTON, *age 53*
PATRICE, *age 42*
YOUNG WOMAN, *undead*

RHODA, *age 49 (to be played by a man)*
PAUL, *age 49*
CAMERAMAN

BUDDY COX, *ageless*
NON, *age 52*

THE CHORUS
JUDE LAW, *played by actor who plays* ORE
JUSTIN TIMBERLAKE, *played by actor who plays* THUS
ZAC EFRON, *played by actor who plays* LAD

Greenwich, Connecticut. 2009

THE AUTHOR WOULD LIKE TO THANK

David Ruttura, Melanie Hopkins, Micah Bucey, Carrie McCrossen, Peter Hagan, Polly Hubbard, Morgan Jenness, Eric Stein, Ben Izzo, Abrams Artists Agency, Ana Mari de Quesada, Wild Project, Matthew Maguire, Elizabeth Margid, The Fordham Alumni Theatre Company, Michael Kimmel, John Johnson, Aaron Rhyne, Morgan Gould, Lark Play Development Center, Kerry O'Malley, Kate Chadwick, Christina Lind, Graham Skipper, John DeLuca, Tom Pecinka, Chris Barlow, Aidan O'Shea, Maria Pizzarello, Katie Riegel, Joey Oliva, Hank & Gaye Ruttura, Hal & Carol Hackett, John & Susan Oliver, the original production cast, crew, and creative team, and, last but not least, Nathan, Meg, and John Oliver, for everything.

PLAYWRIGHT'S NOTE

Forward slashes (" / ") in the text signal for the next character to start saying their line, causing overlapping dialogue.

DEDICATION

for Bonny Boto & Colleen Jordan—
teachers, friends, saviors

ACT ONE

Scene One

(Spotlights on three large wall posters of JUSTIN TIMBERLAKE, JUDE LAW, *and* ZAC EFRON. *They float.)*

(And speak)

JUSTIN TIMBERLAKE: Woe.

JUDE LAW: Woe.

ZAC EFRON: Whoa.

JUDE LAW: What happened here should never happen anywhere.

ZAC EFRON: Why did it happen?

JUDE LAW: It's a tragedy, plain and simple.

JUSTIN TIMBERLAKE: Tragedies always are, man.

ZAC EFRON: Mm. So true.

JUSTIN TIMBERLAKE: Wham, bam, sorry ma'am.

JUDE LAW: Suddenly you've got fistfuls of ash and no pockets.

JUSTIN TIMBERLAKE: Money goes. So do looks.

JUDE LAW: Happiness is suicidal. It's got a gun to its head.

JUSTIN TIMBERLAKE: A hair dryer on the edge of its tub.

JUDE LAW: Happiness barely even gives it a go.

ZAC EFRON: Oh, man, I don't like this. Things like this shouldn't happen.

(*Lights slowly rise to reveal* ELLE'*s bedroom. The posters cover her walls.*)

(ELLE *tears into the room, out of breath and terrified. She's in a one-piece bathing suit, a towel flung over her shoulder.*)

ZAC EFRON: What is it?

JUSTIN TIMBERLAKE: We know.

JUDE LAW: We are sorry. Woe is you.

JUSTIN TIMBERLAKE: Oh!

JUDE LAW: Oh!

ZAC EFRON: Oh!

(ELLE *begins to cry, hyperventilate. She clutches at her throat.*)

JUDE LAW: Speak.

ELLE: I don't know what to do! I went to the pool and Dad was in it and he was dead! (*Sobbing*) I wanted to go swimming, not to see my dad dead!

JUDE LAW: No one will believe you.

ELLE: Oh!

JUSTIN TIMBERLAKE: It will get covered up.

ELLE: Oh!

ZAC EFRON: No one will know.

ELLE: Oh! I'm alone! (*She paces her room, unraveling further.*)

JUDE LAW: Unless.

JUSTIN TIMBERLAKE: Unless.

ZAC EFRON: Unless.

ELLE: Yes?

JUSTIN TIMBERLAKE: Film it.

ZAC EFRON: Document it.

JUSTIN TIMBERLAKE: Seeing

ZAC EFRON: is

JUDE LAW: believing. Make it.

ZAC EFRON: Make it.

JUSTIN TIMBERLAKE: Make it.

JUDE LAW: Make it true. (…) Go!

(ELLE *grabs her video camera, exits.*)

JUDE LAW: Attend this tale: a man is dead.

JUSTIN TIMBERLAKE: A father.

ZAC EFRON: A husband.

JUSTIN TIMBERLAKE: A corporate god.

ZAC EFRON: A maker of mergers.

JUDE LAW: A player of tennis…

ZAC EFRON: Women…

JUDE LAW: And the alto sax.

JUSTIN TIMBERLAKE: A retriever of whiffle balls from the roof.

ZAC EFRON: A provider. Dead.

JUSTIN TIMBERLAKE: Dead.

JUDE LAW: Dead. At the hands of a woman.

ZAC EFRON: His wife.

JUDE LAW: Blood and chlorine.

JUSTIN TIMBERLAKE: Pleasure and pain.

JUDE LAW: His most successful merger of all.

JUSTIN TIMBERLAKE: A husband's decision one night at the office

JUDE LAW: to pat the back of his secretary

ZAC EFRON: and leave his hand there,

JUSTIN TIMBERLAKE: to slide it down her spine,

JUDE LAW: noting her slight scoliosis,

ZAC EFRON: tracing her jaw with a warm thumb,

JUDE LAW: all

ZAC EFRON: the

JUSTIN TIMBERLAKE: while

JUDE LAW: feeling like he hadn't felt in years.

JUSTIN TIMBERLAKE: Invincible.

ZAC EFRON: Young.

JUDE LAW: That decision birthed another:

JUSTIN TIMBERLAKE: That of his wife

ZAC EFRON: to kill

JUSTIN TIMBERLAKE: not just him,

JUDE LAW: but the secretary, too!

JUSTIN TIMBERLAKE: To chop their bodies with the same ax used

JUDE LAW: for chopping down the Christmas pine,

ZAC EFRON: To stuff their parts into the same plastic bags the groceries were brought home in...

JUSTIN TIMBERLAKE: beets,

ZAC EFRON: string cheese,

JUSTIN TIMBERLAKE: ears of sweet corn,

ZAC EFRON: and now arms

JUDE LAW: legs

ZAC EFRON: feet

JUSTIN TIMBERLAKE: actual ears...

JUDE LAW: To bury it all in the backyard…

JUSTIN TIMBERLAKE: all

ZAC EFRON: the

JUDE LAW: while feeling like she hadn't felt in years…

JUSTIN TIMBERLAKE: Invincible.

ZAC EFRON: Young.

JUSTIN TIMBERLAKE: *(Singing)*
"What goes around
Goes around
Goes around
Comes all the way back around…"

(ELLE bursts back into the room, locking the door behind her, camera still in hands.)

ELLE: The bodies.

JUSTIN TIMBERLAKE: Did you get it?

ELLE: They're chopping the bodies. My mom and.

ZAC EFRON: Did you get it?

ELLE: I have to go / back, I have to—

JUDE LAW: Did you get / it?

ELLE: THEY'RE CHOPPING THE BODIES! I HAVE TO STOP THEM!

JUDE LAW: There is nothing you can do out there!

ZAC EFRON: There is

JUSTIN TIMBERLAKE: something you can do

JUDE LAW: up here.

ELLE: *(Hysterical)* What do I do?!

JUSTIN TIMBERLAKE: *(Whispered)* W.

ZAC EFRON: *(Whispered)* W.

JUDE LAW: *(Whispered)* W.

JUSTIN TIMBERLAKE: *(Whispered)* W.

ZAC EFRON: *(Whispered)* W.

JUDE LAW: *(Whispered)* W.

ZAC EFRON: *(Whispered)* W.

JUDE LAW: *(Whispered)* W.

JUSTIN TIMBERLAKE: *(Whispered)* W.

ZAC EFRON: *(Whispered)* W.

JUDE LAW: *(Whispered)* W.

JUSTIN TIMBERLAKE: *(Whispered)* W.

ZAC EFRON: *(Whispered)* W.

JUDE LAW: *(Whispered)* W.

JUSTIN TIMBERLAKE: *(Whispered)* W.

ZAC EFRON: *(Whispered)* W.

JUDE LAW: *(Whispered)* W.

JUSTIN TIMBERLAKE: *(Whispered)* W.

ZAC EFRON: *(Whispered)* W.

JUDE LAW: *(Whispered)* W.

JUSTIN TIMBERLAKE: *(Whispered)* W.

(ELLE *grabs her laptop, hooks the camera into it. She types.)*

JUSTIN TIMBERLAKE: *(Whispered)* W.

ZAC EFRON: *(Whispered)* W.

JUDE LAW: *(Whispered)* W.

ZAC EFRON: Dot.

JUDE LAW: YouTube.

ZAC EFRON: Dot.

JUSTIN TIMBERLAKE: Com. *(…)* Selecting the file.

ZAC EFRON: Clicking "O K."

JUSTIN TIMBERLAKE: O K.

JUDE LAW: O K.

ZAC EFRON: O K.

JUDE LAW: Uploading.

(…)

JUSTIN TIMBERLAKE: Takes a minute.

ZAC EFRON: Things you can do.

JUSTIN TIMBERLAKE: A title.

ELLE: *(Typing)* "S O S"

JUDE LAW: A description.

ELLE: I don't know!

JUDE LAW: Speaks for itself.

ZAC EFRON: Tags?

ELLE: *(Typing)* Murder?

JUSTIN TIMBERLAKE: Mother.

ELLE: *(Whimper)* Father.

ZAC EFRON: Family.

JUSTIN TIMBERLAKE: Betrayal.

ELLE: Revenge.

JUDE LAW: America.

ELLE: Privacy?

JUDE LAW: None.

ELLE: No—it's asking if I want to make the video private or public. "Share your video with the world (Recommended)," or "Private (viewable by you and up to twenty-five people)."

JUDE LAW: Make it public!

JUSTIN TIMBERLAKE: Make it public!

ZAC EFRON: Make it public!

ELLE: I…I don't know. I need to send it to my brother.

ZAC EFRON: Make.

JUDE LAW: It.

JUSTIN TIMBERLAKE: Public. Make.

ZAC EFRON: It.

JUDE LAW: Public. *(Whispered, overlapping)* Make it public!

JUSTIN TIMBERLAKE: *(Whispered, overlapping)* Make it public!

ZAC EFRON: *(Whispered, overlapping)* Make it public!

JUDE LAW: *(Whispered, overlapping)* Make it public!

JUSTIN TIMBERLAKE: *(Whispered, overlapping)* Make it public!

ZAC EFRON: *(Whispered, overlapping)* Make it public!

ELLE: I'm scared.

(…)

ZAC EFRON: It's recommended.

JUSTIN TIMBERLAKE: They recommend it.

JUDE LAW: It's recommended by them.

ELLE: She'll find out!

JUDE LAW: They'll protect you.

ELLE: Who?

ZAC EFRON, JUSTIN TIMBERLAKE, JUDE LAW: The world!

ELLE: It will?

JUSTIN TIMBERLAKE: Yes!

ZAC EFRON: Yes!

JUDE LAW: You're only unsafe when you're unknown.

ELLE: *(Gazing at the screen)* It defaults to public.

JUDE LAW: They're waiting to hear your story.

JUSTIN TIMBERLAKE: This isn't something that ...
happens to everyone.

ZAC EFRON: This happened to you.

JUDE LAW: And only you.

ELLE: To me. And only me.

ZAC EFRON: Submit!

JUDE LAW: Submit!

JUSTIN TIMBERLAKE: Submit!

ELLE: Fuck it. *(Hits a button)* Submit.

Scene Two

(The beautiful backyard of a stunning home. Music)

(THUS stands poolside in a tiny bathing suit, fiddling with the erection that's already tenting his suit. He cleans the swimming pool with a leaf skimmer.)

(CLYT stands on the other side of the pool. She finishes her cigarette and flicks it into the pool, snaps her fingers for THUS and calls his attention to the cigarette butt floating.)

(THUS rushes over to scoop it out.)

(CLYT throws ice cubes from her drink into the pool and orders him to skim them out. This keeps him plenty occupied.)

(CLYT turns to see ETHEL and RHODA approaching from the house, each carrying a copy of The Kite Runner. *She greets them: they hug, air kiss. Discuss why the others will not be joining them. CLYT ushers them to the patio area, on which she has placed several "Afghani" pillows on which they will all sit. Plates of food steam on a table behind them.)*

(Small talk is made. The three women get settled. Drinks are poured. CLYT *lovingly holds her copy of The Kite Runner to her bosom. The music ends, the lights bump up, and:)*

CLYT: Well, I for one just loved this book. Ethel, Rhoda: please help yourselves to the buranee banjan. I want us to really travel to Afghanistan together. In fact, I still think we're too comfortable. How can we properly empathize? We should have sand to throw into each others' eyes. Something. It's a shame the others aren't here, but I suppose everyone has their own set of priorities.

*(*THUS *approaches the table, holding out his empty skimmer.)*

THUS: I tried to get the ice cubes out but they all melted. The pool is going to be freezing. *(He stops in his tracks.)* Guests.

CLYT: Yes, you're right, Thus. We do have guests. Come here, darling: I'd like you to meet Rhoda and Ethel.

THUS: Hello.

CLYT: Don't mumble, dear.

THUS: HELLO!

RHODA: *(Recognizing him)* Are you one of Elle's friends from school?

THUS: Fuck no! She sucks. *(He wanders back over to the pool, continues to clean it.)*

RHODA: Oh! / Well, I…

CLYT: He does go to the same school as Elle, but as fate would have it, Rhoda dear, he's my new friend who helps me with the pool. *(To* THUS*)* What did you say about the pool, Thus?

THUS: Said it was fucked up.

CLYT: And he was right: the pool was effed up. Neglected. So he began to clean it, to give it the love and attention it needed.

(THUS *flexes, intimidates the pool.*)

CLYT: Now, under his tutelage, the pool flourishes, and when he dives in, it welcomes him with adoration and gratitude.

(THUS *smacks the water's surface.* CLYT *giggles.*)

CLYT: That's enough, dear. Run on into the house. What do you say to our guests?

THUS: No diving!

CLYT: No.

THUS: It was nice to meet you?

CLYT: Yes.

THUS: It was nice to meet you. (*He exits.*)

CLYT: I was up half the night crying my eyes out, all because of this magical book. Thus didn't understand, and how could he? He hasn't read it. He hasn't been touched by this lilting, tragic prose. So let's hear from those of us who were. Ethel? What did you think?

ETHEL: I thought it was just lovely.

CLYT: Really. Lovely? It's a brutal book.

ETHEL: But there's...loveliness in the brutality.

CLYT: I didn't think the sodomizing of that little boy was lovely.

ETHEL: Oh my goodness, no!

CLYT: Do you think forced sodomy is lovely?

ETHEL: I don't know what I was thinking. Brutal, yes. Very brutal.

(...)

CLYT: Ethel, name one character from this book.

ETHEL: What?

CLYT: You heard me.

ETHEL: Well, this is silly.

CLYT: Indulge me. Name one.

(ETHEL *glances down at her book, starts to turn it over.*)

CLYT: Don't look at the back cover. Oh, Ethel. For goodness' sake. Did you read the book?

ETHEL: I...I tried. But no. I did not.

CLYT: Oh. I see. Rhoda? Your book looks pristine. Did you not read it either?

RHODA: ...I'm sorry.

CLYT: Of course not; why should you exceed expectation. Well. Where does this leave us? Why did you even come?

ETHEL: Because we're friends!

CLYT: What does that have to do with it?

ETHEL: We wanted to see how you were doing.

RHODA: Since Non left.

ETHEL: You.

RHODA: Yes, left you—oh, / I'm sorry, I.

CLYT: Oh, is that what this is about? The others have sent you both as spies. Spies into broken-hearted territory.

RHODA: Oh, no!

ETHEL: Nothing like that.

CLYT: Her husband's up and left her, run off with some young thing, let's see if she's fallen apart? Lovely. Well, I'm sorry to disappoint you all, but I am thriving.

RHODA: It appears so!

CLYT: I don't like your tone, Rhoda, but I've never liked your tone. What is everyone saying, that I've taken a lover too soon? That he's too young for me?

ETHEL: Heavens, no!

CLYT: Just for the record, and I want you to report this back to the ones who sent you: I exhaust him. Tell them.

ETHEL: Okay.

RHODA: Oh—okay.

CLYT: My husband has disappeared, yes. But my life has reappeared. My life. I'm cooking again!

RHODA: Oh, yes!

ETHEL: Looks delicious!

CLYT: The air is scented, the pool is a magnificent blue, and I just read a fantastic book I was hoping to discuss today with my—why do you two keep glancing behind me? Is there something wrong?

ETHEL: It's nothing.

RHODA: Nothing at all!

CLYT: What is going on?

(RHODA *exchanges a look with* ETHEL.)

ETHEL: How is Elle handling everything?

CLYT: Oh, girls: do you ever look at your children and wonder if they actually came from you?

ETHEL: Oh, yes.

RHODA: Mine didn't.

CLYT: I had them put her on an anti-depressant. I have to mash it up and put it in her food, like she's a dog with ringworm. What is with the little looks you two are sharing!

(…)

RHODA: *(Here goes nothing)* So Non just…ran off?

CLYT: Yes.

RHODA: Did he leave. A note?

CLYT: A / note?

ETHEL: *(To* RHODA*)* His business.

RHODA: What about his business? He just dropped everything?

CLYT: Yes, Rhoda, he dropped everything.

RHODA: It just doesn't seem like him!

CLYT: Have you no decency, Rhoda? How many drinks did you have before you came here?

RHODA: None! I /—one! Just one!

CLYT: Interrogating me about my husband when / you're under the influence.

RHODA: It's just to loosen my / neck, that's all.

CLYT: My God, Rhoda, it's two-thirty in the afternoon.

RHODA: *(Breaking point)* My Kirsten forwarded me a video!

CLYT: A video. Yes?

ETHEL: …that Elle posted on a website.

CLYT: Yes, a website? *(…)* This must go faster.

ETHEL: YouTube.

CLYT: What did she post? Is she naked?

RHODA: No.

CLYT: Is she doing some sort of opiate?

RHODA: No. Nothing like that.

CLYT: Singing? I know she dabbles.

RHODA: No. / No.

CLYT: Well, out with it!

RHODA: I can't say it.

CLYT: Ethel? Will you tell me? Will you look me in the eye?

ETHEL: It's a video of you.

CLYT: Of me? What am I—?

ETHEL: Oh, my / goodness, I'm...

CLYT: *(Slamming her hand down)* WHAT!

RHODA: Don't you know? I mean, really! Don't you?!

(...)

CLYT: Oh.

RHODA: Please don't make us say it.

CLYT: I'd like to hear you say it. I'd like to punish you both for coming to Book Club unprepared. But I won't.

RHODA: Thank you, Clyt.

CLYT: So you both have seen it. You went on YouTube and you found it.

RHODA: Well, Kirsten found it somehow, I guess someone had sent it to her. You know kids and their little grapevines...

ETHEL: ...text messages, notes in the lockers...

RHODA: Social butterflies. So she sent it to me, and I / sent it...

ETHEL: She sent it to me. I asked Patrick if he'd seen it, and he had. Someone had it on in Spanish class earlier that day.

RHODA: Really! In Spanish class?

ETHEL: Yes, after watching it a couple of times, the teacher had them translate it and act it out in Spanish.

RHODA: That's progressive teaching!

ETHEL: Well, you know, they'll do anything to keep the kids engaged these days.

RHODA: Oh, I know, no child / left behind!

CLYT: Excuse me. How many people did you forward it to after you watched it?

(…)

ETHEL: Well. I mean, I sent it to Judy…

CLYT: *(Pointing to where Judy usually sits)* Uh huh: Judy. Who else?

ETHEL: And Trina…

CLYT: *(Pointing to another chair)* Trina: check.

ETHEL: O K, I also sent it to Lynette because in stripper cardio this morning she was the only one who hadn't… you know. She was going to look it up anyway; this / was just easier.

CLYT: And Lynette. Lynette, whom we've always suspected to be teaching herself to read through this Club. You said you were my friends.

ETHEL: We are! That's why we're here!

CLYT: Yet neither of you thought to send this clip to me. Did you?

ETHEL: Well. I.

RHODA: I mean, you're in the video. I mean, you've "seen" it!

CLYT: That, Rhoda, is the stupidest thing you have ever said, and your canon is illustrious. I need to see this video for myself. I'm getting my computer.

ETHEL: This is a family matter; we should / really be getting home.

CLYT: Oh, no. You two stay right where you are. I want to watch this in the company of friends. *(She runs off into the house.)*

ETHEL: We need to get out of here fast.

RHODA: We can't just leave, can we?

ETHEL: Of course we can. Get up! Quick, before she gets back!

(The two grab their things.)

RHODA: The Kite Runner!

ETHEL: Leave it!

(CLYT re-enters, carrying her laptop.)

CLYT: Not so fast, ladies. You sit back down here with your good friend Clyt.

(She sits again, gestures for them to join her. They do so. CLYT opens her laptop and begins typing.)

CLYT: What's the title? *(...)* What's the title?!

ETHEL: "S O S"!

(CLYT types in the title.)

CLYT: "This video may contain content that is inappropriate for some users ..."

ETHEL: I flagged it as inappropriate.

CLYT: Well, thank you, Ethel; I appreciate that. O K, shush. I'm watching.

(The video begins. We only hear audio from the computer.)

ELLE: *(V O)* Mom? Where did you—go—you—oh my god—you're—

CLYT: *(V O)* Elle?

ELLE: *(V O)*
Mommy? Oh dear God.   CLYT: *(V O. A little ways
Oh dear God   away)*

in heaven, come
and save me. What
are you doing?!

Oh god, oh god, oh
god.

She killed him.
She killed my
father. She killed
my father. Oh my
God. Oh my God.
No! No!

Mommy? Did you
just say mommy?
Did you just call
me mommy?

I am putting them
in the ground
where they belong,
dear, just—
listen, come here—
I'll—

Elle! Elle!
(*Closer now*)
Please come here!
Mommy is here now,
she's here now,
and she's not
going to hurt you!
(*Far away*)
Don't run! You're my
child!

(*The sounds of struggle are heard. The camera is dropped.*)

ELLE: (*V O. Also far*)   CLYT: (*V O*)
Get off of me!   I love you!
Stop it!
I hate you! I   I love you! Don't
hate you!   say that!

ELLE: (*V O*) You should have died!

CLYT: (*V O*) I am just! I am just! I am ju—

(*The video ends.*)

ETHEL: Well. Her bias is certainly present.

(*CLYT pitches forward, grabs the table, clutches her womb.*)

CLYT: Oh. She is against me. She is from me yet she is against me. *(Falling into her chair)* What do people think? People have seen it? The school, the book club, the museum board?

(ETHEL and RHODA nod.)

CLYT: Am I ruined? *(...)* There is no one here. Am I—I am frightening? To women? To my own kind?

ETHEL: We're here.

CLYT: *(Wiping the only tear that fell)* Yes. Yes, you are here. You aren't frightened of me?

ETHEL: No!

RHODA: Yes?

CLYT: Oh, girls. This is a time for friendship. For sisterhood.

ETHEL: So it's true.

CLYT: Yes.

ETHEL: You killed him.

CLYT: Them.

RHODA: Them!

CLYT: The mistress too. She was with child.

RHODA: His?

CLYT: *(Sharp)* Yes, Rhoda: his.

RHODA: Oh, dear.

CLYT: *(Wipes crumbs from the table)* I knew her; she worked for him. He came to me. He said, his assistant, she was in trouble, she was in a bad spot, was young and stupid with some man from a bar, and her family had thrown her out, a disgrace. He appealed to my—to the charity in my heart. I opened my home to her. I ran her baths, I washed her clothes and folded them, full of concern for her, for she was a young woman;

she was no mother. I cared for this girl. Every day she
would swim. We watched her, Non and I. From the
kitchen, from our bedroom, from the driveway, where
we were taking out the garbage together for the first.
(...) I thought we were—closer, watching her swim,
worrying about her. I thought that for six full days,
for six warm swims. And then on the seventh day he
joined her in the pool. He joined her in the pool and I
saw them together, and it was so. Small, but, suddenly
clear. I was in the kitchen, in the bedroom, in the
driveway; I was everywhere at once, and I dropped
it all—the dishes, the laundry, the garbage—three
selves becoming one—and I walked to the pool and I
drowned them. I flipped the switch for the automated
pool cover to roll out. The pool was half covered by
the time they realized. And then it was a real race, let
me tell you. She was screaming, crying, pounding,
but Non—Non was just floating there, looking up at
me. Right into my eyes, even. He looked at me for the
first time in many years. I saw the whites of his eyes.
He wasn't scared at all; he was open to me. He smiled
a little. And I went back to the controls and I flooded
the pool, mainly so he'd stop smiling as if this was just
another thing he'd wanted and, as always, received.
I didn't turn off the water until I saw their bodies
smacking against the cover. The yard flooded; the grass
died with them. These events, they must be bled out.
Washed in rivers of red out to the seas to re-hydrate
the earth. (...) My son. It will come just as easily to him.
My god. He will kill me. Tell me, this video: it can be
viewed by anyone, anywhere?

ETHEL: Anywhere they can get the Internet.

RHODA: Which, let's face it, is everywhere these days!

CLYT: Oh, girls! I will be ended!

(*YouTube comments:*)

A: First 2 comment!! LOL

B: Whoa tho that was 2 crazy 2 b true. Was that a joke?
R U 4 real? Email me & let me no.

C: What a sorry state we are in if this is what we r
watching

D: what would you rather watch?

E: How about the economy seriously or iran or
something that might in some way effect us

F: U can't watch an economy dipshit!!!

G: Okay I can't decide what's happening in this vid.
My friend forwarded it and I've watched it a hundred
times and forwarded it to more people and no one
knows. Is it a joke? I don't think it's very funny, but I
don't think much of what's on here is funny. That's just
me, take it or leave it.

H: Did someone actually get killed? Why isn't this on
the news?

I: Do U need help???

J: You can totally watch an economy—its called stocks
and airplanes and hotels and basically anywhere
anyone wants to be is empty—thats what you watch

K: What happened at the end? Is this part of a series?
Can't find the beginning—help!

L: Thumbs down. Next!

M: Fuck you, thumbs down. THUMBS UP BITCH!

N: YO THEY CHOPPIN THOSE BODIES UP...not cool
but kinda funny ???

O: im offended even if this is a joke its not funny to
make fun of abusive homes how many kids live in
fear of their parents id rather my kids respect me than
fear me just my opinion but its true even if this is a

joke its not funny nothing to laugh about this is really happening lots of other places and theyre not laughing

P: :(this is sad i'm sorry i watched this i don't know why but i am :(:(:(

Q: Hey Debbie Downer, it's a fucking JOKE. Some Blair Witch shit, it's easy, you take a camera in the woods and fuck up some stuff and everybody falls for it. DOn't bring your fucking statistics here. Everybody wants to be offended every moment of every fucking day like some dcrybaby but THIS IS LIFE and you MAKE YOUR OWN CIRCUMSTANCES. IT's NOBODY's FAULT BUTTHEIR OWN.

R: Hey girl i know your sad but let me see a little smile next time. When do we get to see more of you? want to see that face light up wit a smile.

Scene Three

(ELLE's *bedroom*)

(ELLE *sits on her bed, filming another video.*)

ELLE: Hello everyone. It's me, Elle. I'm here to let you know this isn't a joke. It's real. And it's so horrible. Like, when I was younger and I thought about things I never thought about this. Please believe me? My mom really did kill my dad, and she had no right to do that. She thinks she does, but she is wrong. She had no right. (*Collects herself*) I just want to thank everyone: all of you who watched my last video and left a comment. I did read all of them, even the mean ones. But to those of you that were nice, thank you for your love and support and for saying I'm pretty. That was really nice and it means a lot to me. (*She starts to cry, uploads the video. She climbs onto her bed, lies down.*) Oh god, oh god, oh god.

JUDE LAW: Oh Elle!

JUSTIN TIMBERLAKE: Oh Elle!

ZAC EFRON: Oh Elle!

JUDE LAW: The world has raised its hand

JUSTIN TIMBERLAKE: turned its rings around

ZAC EFRON: smacked the crap out of you.

JUDE LAW: Oh, how you suffer.

ZAC EFRON: Bad stuff.

JUSTIN TIMBERLAKE: It happens to good people.

ELLE: Everything hurts. I wish it was all a dream.

JUDE LAW: You are so bright.

ZAC EFRON: So smart.

JUSTIN TIMBERLAKE: So promising.

ELLE: Or maybe I'm just crazy. Maybe this is life and it sucks and I'm gonna be fucking nuts during all of it.

JUDE LAW: Nice work if you can get it.

JUSTIN TIMBERLAKE: Some people would kill to be nuts.

(ELLE *buries her head in her pillow, sobs.*)

ZAC EFRON: *(Singing)* My girl…

JUSTIN TIMBERLAKE: *(Singing)* My girl…

JUDE LAW: *(Singing)* My girl…

(ELLE *emerges from her pillow.*)

ELLE: My dad used to sing all the time.

ZAC EFRON: What would he sing?

ELLE: Actually, I don't remember him singing ever. I remember him shaving. I used to watch him, when I was young, and I'd cross my fingers that he wouldn't cut himself.

ZAC EFRON: And what would he say?

ELLE: What?

ZAC EFRON: When you'd cross your fingers?

ELLE: Oh. Well, I did it behind him. I mean, he knew, he just didn't. *(Opens her computer, reads a few comments)* "When do we get to see more of you? want to see that face light up wit a smile." Who are these people?

JUSTIN TIMBERLAKE: People who can help.

ZAC EFRON: People who care.

ELLE: Where is Ore? Everyone's watching it but him.

JUDE LAW: Perhaps he's busy.

ELLE: He's bored out of his mind last I checked.

ZAC EFRON: Maybe it got busy.

(...)

ELLE: Oh my god, is he dead?! Do you—? *(Turns to them, panicked)*

Know? Is he? No, don't tell me. Don't tell me.

JUSTIN TIMBERLAKE: We don't know.

ELLE: Oh god, that would be too—I'd, I'd die, I'd.

JUSTIN TIMBERLAKE: Oh, Elle.

JUDE LAW: Oh, Elle.

ZAC EFRON: Oh, Elle.

ELLE: Please don't be dead. Please don't be dead. Please oh please. *(She watches another YouTube video.)*

ORE: *(V O. Outside noise heard as well)* Hey, sis, it's me, coming to you live from scenic Sadr City. Just wanted to say hey. Hope you're doing good. Hope school's good and stuff. Um, love you, miss you. Oh, wait, this fucker / wants to say hi.

(Sounds of camera shuffling.)

LAD: *(V O)* "Hey, sis." I love you and miss you...

(ELLE *clicks a button, starts the video back again.*)

ORE: *(V O)* ...school's good and stuff. Um, love you, miss you.

(The video clicks back.)

ORE: *(V O)* ...stuff. Um, love you, miss you.

(Again)

ORE: *(V O)* ...Love you, miss you.

(Again)

ORE: *(V O)* ...good and stuff. Um, love you, miss you.

(There's some fumbling at the door. ELLE slams her computer shut just in time as THUS barges into her room.)

THUS: You're in trouble, young lady.

ELLE: Young lady?

THUS: Yuh huh, / young lady.

ELLE: What the hell, you're my age.

(THUS sighs.)

THUS: You're in trouble, young lady.

ELLE: Get the hell out of my room.

THUS: I'll get the hell out of your gay room / when I'm good and ready...

ELLE: What are you doing here?

THUS: Come to get you.

ELLE: Get me?

THUS: Get you. There's a doctor lady here and your mom / wants you to see her.

ELLE: My mom—she couldn't even come up here herself. She had to send you.

THUS: You guys need a man around here to take care of things.

ELLE: What about school?

THUS: What about it?

ELLE: Are you still—going to go? Am I going to see you in the, / in the hallway?

THUS: Fuck school. I gotta run this house.

ELLE: Listen: I know we aren't, like, friends or anything, but can we talk about this? I mean, you clean pools, right?

THUS: Yeah.

ELLE: And what's normally in the pools you have to clean?

THUS: Leaves. Dead birds.

ELLE: Uh huh. So when they sent you here to clean our pool, what was in it?

THUS: Puke. Blood.

ELLE: *(Wavering)* Uh huh.

THUS: Your dad and some girl.

ELLE: And what did you think?

THUS: Big job.

ELLE: Big job?!

THUS: Overtime.

ELLE: My mom had just killed them. Which is wrong!

THUS: Eh. Depends on how you look at it.

ELLE: Um, there's only one way.

THUS: I'm a little older than you, / so I've learned…

ELLE: Two years. Two years older than me.

THUS: I wasn't just cleaning the pool. I was making things right. Not every day you get paid to make things right.

ELLE: Oh god!

(ELLE *buries her face in her pillow, sobs.* THUS *sits on her bed.*)

THUS: *(His best attempt at fatherly)* Do you want to talk about it?

ELLE: Oh god, get up! I don't want your balls on my bed!

THUS: You like it.

(ELLE *kicks at* THUS *until he stands.*)

ELLE: Aren't you scared? She could kill you!

THUS: Not possible. I could take her.

ELLE: My dad was stronger than you and she killed him. She kills men, men who disappoint her. You're dropping out of school, where are you going to work, sweeping a / broom when some wind chimes break in fucking Aisle 6…

THUS: Or, or, or maybe everything will be awesome for me. Do you ever think of that?

ELLE: *(Throwing her hands up)* No. No, I do not.

THUS: You obviously wouldn't know this, but things just kind of happen for hot people, and you don't even need all of it sometimes. You're like, whoa, sweet car, hot chick, and a lot of money, all for me? I mean, fine, whatever, I'll take it if you want to give it to me, all I was doing was sitting here eating a sandwich.

ELLE: Then my brother will kill you. I've got you on video and Ore will / see it and he won't be happy.

THUS: Yeah, but he's not here now!

ELLE: No, he's in the fucking army. You know / that, right?

THUS: Shut up. Shut the / fuck up.

ELLE: You hear me, numb-nuts? Or am I using too many big words? Let me make it easier. Brother. / Man. Man with gun.

THUS: Shut up. Shut the fuck up. I'm gonna—shut you the fuck up.

ELLE: Man with gun who'll be mad at you. He's gonna come back here after killing a bunch of people, what's one more idiot like you!

(THUS *hits* ELLE *in the stomach and smacks her across the face. She cries out, falls back. He grabs her neck in a one-handed chokehold, forces her down onto her bed.*)

THUS: I AM NOT AN IDIOT! I'M YOUR NEW DAD, THAT's WHAT I AM! That's right. You'll ask me for Christmas presents. You'll learn to drive in my car. And I'll walk you down the aisle, if you get married. (*He lets go of her.*) Nobody's killing me. (*He pulls down his bathing suit, rubs his genitals on her comforter.*) Now my balls are on your fucking bed.

(ELLE *faints.*)

(*YouTube comments*)

A: wait y is she crying?its sad 2 see her cry=(

B: It's so sad… She's such a strong 'girl' and yet it's even hard for her to be 'strong' over and over again… like when she trys to laugh… :'/

C: SSSSSHHHHHHHH IT's OKAY

D: Because teens always tell the truth about their families—we trust what they say…sarcasm OFF

E: Fucking sycho bitch why don't you fuck off!

F: ROTFLMAO!!! What is this shit? Is this real?

G: UMMMMMM think about it—if this was real why would it be on YouTube before it was anywhere else? Yah thought so

H: WTF is your problem? You think she's lying???

I: Do U need someone to come get U?

J: You'll be 18 before you know it! Emancipate!

K: Im just saying theres 2 sides to every coin—what if she's just pissed at her mom or something—she could get in serious trouble—girls are always doing sshit like this

Scene Four

(The backyard)

(DR EDITH HAMILTON sits in one of the pool chairs. CLYT is setting down a pitcher of lemonade next to a tray with four glasses on it.)

(THUS enters, carrying ELLE, who is slumped over his shoulder.)

CLYT: Oh! Is she?

THUS: Fainted. At least she's quiet.

(THUS dumps ELLEr on a pool chair.)

CLYT: Be—careful, dear.

(THUS sits in his own pool chair. CLYT goes to ELLE, sits with her, touches her forehead.)

CLYT: Elle? Elle, dear?

(CLYT leans in, kisses ELLE's forehead. ELLE stirs, sees CLYT hovering above her.)

CLYT: You took quite a / fall!

ELLE: What?! Get the fuck away from me!

(ELLE *pushes and lashes out at* CLYT, *swiping her across the face.* CLYT *crumples away from* ELLE, *clutching at her ear.* THUS *and* DR HAMILTON *both stand, but* CLYT *raises a hand to stop them.*)

CLYT: I'm all right. I'm all right.

DR HAMILTON: You're bleeding.

(CLYT *glances at the fingers with which she was covering her ear. They're bloody.*)

CLYT: Well, she. She got my earring.

(ELLE *holds up her own hand, discovers* CLYT'*s earring in it.*)

ELLE: Oh—/ shit, I.

CLYT: I'm all right. Goodness, though, that hurt.

(THUS *and* DR HAMILTON *tentatively sit. She goes back to the table and applies a napkin to her ear.*)

CLYT: Lemonade, Doctor Hamilton?

DR HAMILTON: Oh, yes, please!

CLYT: Thus, lemonade?

THUS: Mmm.

CLYT: Elle?

ELLE: You made lemonade?

CLYT: Life handed us lemons!

ELLE: Life handed me lemons, you bitch!

CLYT: (*To* DR HAMILTON) I like this: dialogue. This is healthy. (*To* ELLE)

I'm so happy to see you, Elle, out of the house and away from your computer, in the company of others, in the sun. You look as if you could one day be healthy. What do you say? How about a nice cold glass?

ELLE: I'd rather drink a stranger's piss.

CLYT: All right, I won't force it. I am respecting her wishes. She'd rather a stranger's urine… (*To* ELLE) …a stranger's urine.

ELLE: (*To* DR HAMILTON) Help me!

CLYT: Oh, what luck! That's exactly why Doctor Hamilton is here.

DR HAMILTON: Hello, Elle. It's me, Doctor Hamilton. I knew you when you were six. Do you remember me? I came over for dinner with my then-husband Albert, and you danced for us at the table for a good hour. You and your brother: you acted out "The Rescuers." We laughed and cheered and prayed you wouldn't stop. Ever. Do you remember?

ELLE: Um, no. No I do not. Have you seen my video?

DR HAMILTON: I have, yes, at your mother's request.

ELLE: And?

DR HAMILTON: And I'm greatly troubled by it.

ELLE: Thank you!

DR HAMILTON: The part that troubles me the most is when you say to your mother: "You should have died."

(ELLE *stands.*)

ELLE: What?!

CLYT: Elle, sit down.

DR HAMILTON: It's quite all right; I welcome standing. (*Rising as well*) Let's talk.

ELLE: Who are you?

DR HAMILTON: I beg your pardon?

ELLE: What are your credentials? Where / did you graduate from?

CLYT: Elle!

DR HAMILTON: Is college something you are interested in, Elle?

(…)

ELLE: I'm sorry. Are we conversing? Because / I don't know.

CLYT: *(To* ELLE*)* Elle, please sit. The reason I asked you to join us for analysis / today is that we…

ELLE: Join you—he / dragged me here!

CLYT: I understand that you need to act out, that you need to make some sense of what happened, and I am available to you if you have any questions, or if you'd / care to talk…

ELLE: Questions!

CLYT: Edith!

DR HAMILTON: Go ahead, Clyt.

CLYT: I would like to apologize to you, Elle, for how unavailable I was to you for, well, for the majority of your life. I was not capable of it, and I hope you can forgive me, your father / did some very…

ELLE: You don't get to blame him for everything.

CLYT: Well, I suppose you're right. *(…)* Do you remember what you said to me that night you came home early and found me digging the graves?

ELLE: You know, as fondly as I think about that, I just / can't remember.

CLYT: I do. You said, "Mommy." A child's voice in the black night: "Mommy?" You hadn't called me that in years. I'd do it all over again if it got you to call me that just one more time. I'd do it a / hundred times over.

ELLE: You are the most fucked up person I know.

CLYT: Well. I took a chance, I opened my heart to you, and I accept your response.

ELLE: Say you're sorry.

CLYT: No.

ELLE: *(Small child)* Be sorry!

CLYT: But I'm not.

ELLE: *(Crying)* Why not?

CLYT: Your father betrayed me.

ELLE: Oh, please.

CLYT: Did you not see the other woman in our house?

ELLE: Yes, it sucked, I know!

CLYT: *(Laugh)* It sucked. *(To* DR HAMILTON*)* It "sucked"!
(To ELLE*)* Yes: it sucked.

ELLE: I hated him for bringing her here.

CLYT: As did I.

ELLE: No, but I still loved him!

CLYT: As did I!

ELLE: Well, great way to show it. Kill him.

CLYT: I agree.

ELLE: OH MY GOD! NO! DON'T AGREE! You took
him away from me. I'll never have a dad again.

CLYT: There are things you don't know.

ELLE: So tell me!

CLYT: No. You are a child. Enjoy that; it's the last gift I
can give you.

ELLE: Fuck you.

CLYT: Oh!

ELLE: No, fuck you.

CLYT: Oh, Edith, I need your support!

DR HAMILTON: *(Taking her hand)* You can do it. Trust
yourself.

ELLE: *(To* DR HAMILTON*)* She's scared because my brother's gonna see the video and he's / gonna be pissed.

CLYT: What you did was dangerous. Do you think your brother will react reasonably after your provocation? No. Men are brutes, they snap / and they lash out...

ELLE: Oh, yes, because you were incredibly / thoughtful...

CLYT: Mommy could be killed.

ELLE: Good!

(DR HAMILTON *throws her hands in the air.*)

DR HAMILTON: Highly troubling!

CLYT: How can you say that? You are my child.

ELLE: You don't know anything about me!

CLYT: *(To* DR HAMILTON*)* I learned early on that she preferred her father to me. I bled rivers when she was born. The doctor said she couldn't wait to be rid of me.

ELLE: He loved me; he bought me my video camera because he knew that / I wanted to make movies.

CLYT: He bought that because I told him you wanted it.

ELLE: You're lying.

CLYT: He did not know what to do with you. He was always with your brother, and when Ore was older he'd take him on business trips. He called them Boys' Trips. Do you remember?

ELLE: Yes. So?

CLYT: Do you also remember running down the driveway after them, crying your eyes out? You'd fight me, push me away, like a demon. Funny thing is: I envied you your childhood abandon. I too wanted to pound my fists on the driveway as the Boys rode away.

ELLE: He loved you, too.

CLYT: *(Fierce)* If you're that stupid then I have failed you.

ELLE: On the Internet they think I'm right. They say poor Elle, and you'll get through, just take it one day at a time, and that I deserve / to have a normal life.

CLYT: Well, I'm so happy that you've finally found people to care about you, strangers / on the Internet.

ELLE: They do!

CLYT: Perhaps I should make a video, too, and see how it makes you feel!

(…)

DR HAMILTON: Perhaps you should.

CLYT: What?

DR HAMILTON: It could be a response. A public statement.

CLYT: You know, Edith, that's not a bad idea. Come to think of it.

DR HAMILTON: Come to think of it, Clyt: come to think of it. Yes.

CLYT: Yes. That does seem to be what's required here, doesn't it, Edith? The voice of reason. The voice of a mother. The context. *(To* ELLE*)* You're not the only one with a story to tell the world, Elle dear.

THUS: Can I be in the video, please!

CLYT: But of course. It wouldn't be a real response without the man of the house in it.

THUS: That's right. *(To* ELLE*)* Your brother won't come around here. He won't come to my house.

CLYT: Hear, hear!

THUS: Here, here! *(He pours his lemonade around the perimeter of the pool.)* This is my grass, this is my water, this is my woman. He won't be coming here. *(He drops to his knees, pounds the ground.)*

CLYT: No, he won't.

THUS: Gimme. *(He grabs her waist, buries his face in it, roars into her. He grabs at her breasts and she moans.)* *(Muffled in her crotch)* Mine, mine, mine. *(To the others)* We're gonna go fuck now.

(CLYT and THUS exit. DR HAMILTON finishes writing her prescription.)

ELLE: I guess everyone has their price.

DR HAMILTON: *(Stopping)* You know. There was another part of your video that resonated for me. After viewing it, I realized clearly that my current husband has gambled away all of our savings on horses. I've spent my life listening to people's problems and I have nothing to show for it. I'm going to have to work until I die, listening to the rancor. Last night while Theodore was sleeping I just, I just rested my pillow over his face and pressed down ever so gently. He stirred, and I was frightened and I stopped, but. There was a thrill. I could feel my blood—push against my skin. *(Checking her watch)* Well. I'd say this was about an hour.

(YouTube video)

(Ext. The house—day)

(CLYT opens the front door, addresses the camera directly.)

CLYT: Well hello, YouTube…and welcome to my home. Please, come in!

(Camera steps into the foyer.)

CLYT: Oh, but take off your shoes first! Your feet are very dirty!

(…)

RHODA: *(O C. Whispered)* Me?

CLYT: Yes, Rhoda.

(Camera shuffles, image blurs. Cut to: Int. Living room—moments later)

(CLYT sits on the sofa.)

CLYT: Please: make yourself comfortable. Sit a spell, why don't you?

(Camera joins her on the sofa.)

CLYT: I'm glad you came. I feel like we got off on the wrong foot, and if you give me a chance you'll find that there's more to me than what you saw in my daughter's highly-edited, Michael Moore-influenced short film. You'll see that I am a woman of principle and integrity, a woman equal parts tigress and kitten, a proud mother, a devoted friend, and a sensational lover. I think we'll be fast friends; I'm sure of it.

(Cut to: Int. Kitchen—moments later)

CLYT: Here we are in the kitchen. I just love rolling up my sleeves and cooking big meals for my family and friends.

(Cut to: Int. Bathroom—moments later)

(CLYT is scrubbing the shower.)

CLYT: Oh, you caught me! Neat freak! Guilty as charged!

(Cut to: Int. living room—moments later)

CLYT: *(At the mantle which is covered with framed photographs, one of which still has a price tag on it)* This is my son, who is heroically serving his country overseas. Look at how handsome he is. *(To the camera)* Mommy is so proud of you, dear, and she loves you very much. *(To the mantle)* Here he is at his graduation. And here he is on his way to the prom—I was a chaperone, but folks thought I was his date! This was in Italy on one of our vacations. *(Gestures to a smaller photograph at the end of the mantle)* And here's my daughter, who many of you have already "met6." The odds were certainly stacked high against her as a child. I nourished her, coaxed her out of the shadows as far as I could, but let's face it: some people like the darkness and the cold.

(Cut to: Ext. The deck—moments later)

CLYT: Not me! *(She holds up a drink.)* Mojito?

(Cut to: Ext. garden—moments later)

(CLYT is digging in the garden.)

CLYT: I think I need a doctor to look at my thumbs— they're green!

(Cut to: Int. A restaurant—later)

(CLYT sits at a table with ETHEL and RHODA.)

CLYT: Here I am, out on the town with the girls. Say hello, girls.

ETHEL: Hello.

RHODA: What / a nice...

CLYT: I maintain an active social life. I simply must or I'd start to feel like the fogey I am! *(To a passing waiter)* Could I have another fizzy water, please? Thank you, Matteo. *(To camera)* I also believe in rewarding good service. He will get an excellent tip.

ETHEL: That wasn't our waiter.

CLYT: It wasn't?

(Cut to: Int. a movie theater—later)

(CLYT and THUS sit next to each other.)

CLYT: Date Night is vital when you're in a committed relationship and raising a family together. Thus and I adore going to movies with Goldie Hawn's Daughter in them.

MOVIE PATRON: *(O C)* Sssshhhh!

CLYT: *(Whispered)* I wonder if Goldie Hawn and her Daughter ever see things a little differently! Hmmm?

MOVIE PATRON: *(O C)* Ssssshhhhh!!

THUS: You want to die tonight, punk?!

(Camera shuffles, image blurs.)

(Cut to: Int. A church—later)

(CLYT is in line to shake hands with the MINISTER on the way out of the church.)

CLYT: I'm also a woman of faith. I don't know where I'd be without the man upstairs.

(CLYT shakes hands with the MINISTER.)

CLYT: Wonderful as always, Father.

MINISTER: We're so pleased you joined us this Sunday. We love new members!

(…)

CLYT: *(To camera)* Ha! Ha! Oh, Father!

(Cut to: Ext. The house—later)

(CLYT stands at the front door again.)

CLYT: Well, thank you so much for coming by and spending some quality time with me. I hope you saw that I'm very much a whole and complicated woman with a good heart. Yes, I killed my husband and his mistress. But I ask of you: didn't that bathroom look like heaven once it had been scrubbed free of its offensive filth? I've got news for you: Heaven's here on Earth.

(An egg timer buzzes off-camera.)

CLYT: Oh! That'd be my muffins. Don't be a stranger now, you hear? *(She closes the door.)*

(Cut to black)

(YouTube comments)

A: let's see more of ya & yur muffins

B: This is utter garbage and I love it. She can't be serious!!!

C: I'd like to see u fight me

D: LOLOLOLOLOL THIS IS GREAT! I'M SENDING THIS TO EVERYONE I KNOW!

E: Someone seriously needs to call Oprah and get this woman on. When she looks right at the camera she scares me.

F: You've got cum on your lip i think it looks like it anybody else see it? Hahahaaa

G: I think she's pretty!

H: sry once someone has cheated the rules get thrown out the window—i dont blame her—maybe if more men knew this was what would happen to them they would think twice before cheating

I: You think it's okay to just kill people? You don't get it, do you?

J: I DON'T KNOW MAYBE I'M IN THE MINORITY, BUT SHE SEems to be living the high life w/ a hotter guy and a nice house and lots of $$$, everyone's just jealous!

K: KILLER MILF
KILLER MILF
KILLER MILF

L: will u marry me? a rose 4 u

================================<@

Scene Five

(ELLE's *bedroom*)

(ELLE *is sitting at her computer.*)

ELLE: What the hell! Her video is, like, blowing up! She's got almost as many views as mine and the majority of her comments are positive. (...) Is she right?

JUDE LAW: No!

JUSTIN TIMBERLAKE: No!

ZAC EFRON: No!

ELLE: What if she's right? What if she was allowed to kill him? Am I wrong? (...) I must be wrong.

ZAC EFRON: Oh, no, don't say that!

ELLE: No, I'm going to say it.

ZAC EFRON: But it's not / helpful right—

ELLE: Don't tell me what I can and can't say! (*She reaches for her camera, aims it at herself, presses the record button. Into the camera*) Are you there? It's me, Elle. I just want you to know that
I see all the things you're doing for my mom and I just wanted to ask you why. No, not why. How. How could you? How could you abandon me when I need you most?

(*YouTube comments*)

A: U forgot to swallow...lol

B: scaryshit man

C: I LOVE IT THIS IS BETTER THAN TV

D: That's what I said to your mom last night.

E: Y U GOTTA BE LIKE THAT? DAMN.

F: I don't know, I hear her, I agree with her for like one second and then I remember what she did and it's hard to still agree

G: Crazy bitch! You were his wife and you promised to love honor and obey and you broke your promise!

H: Search "crazyhorselondon" to see ppl getting killed

I: lesbian

J: lonely?
click here to find love
click here to find love
click here to find love

K: Ha man you forgot the last part of that is 'til death do you part, and it did—so the point is moott...

Scene Six

(In darkness we hear:)

ELLE: *(V O)*
She killed him.
She killed my
father. She killed
my father. Oh my
God. Oh my God.
No! No!

CLYT: *(V O)*
Elle! Elle!
(Closer now)
Please come here!
Mommy is here now,
she's here now,
and she's not
going to hurt you!
(Far away) Don't run!
You're my child!

(Lights up on an army tent)

(ORE is on the ground, in fatigues, staring up, a gun in his hand. LAD sits near him, also in fatigues, watching ELLE's video on a laptop. From the computer we hear:)

ELLE: *(V O. Also far)*   CLYT: *(V O)*
Get off of me!   I love you!
Stop it!
I hate you! I   I love you! Don't
hate you!   say that!

ELLE: *(V O)* You should have died!

CLYT: *(V O)* I am just! I am just! I am ju—

LAD: I love when she— *(He clicks a button.)*

ELLE: *(V O)* …have died!

CLYT: *(V O)* I am just! I am just! I am ju—

LAD: "I am just! I am just!" Fuck. Gives me the. *(Sighs)*
We came here but the war's back there. First kill we
see and it's on… *(Jabs a finger angrily at the computer)* …
fuckin' T V.

ORE: Not T V.

LAD: YouTube.

ORE: Not YouTube, my life.

LAD: That, too.

ORE: Unnnnh.

LAD: Sorry. I'll stop.

(LAD closes the laptop. ORE brings the gun to his head.)

LAD: Whoa! Hey! Hey!

ORE: What?

LAD: *(Crawling to him)*
What are you doing?

ORE: *(Rolling away from him)*
This.

LAD: No!

ORE: Yes!

LAD: No, no, no! What the fuck are you doing? Put that down, man!

Just—chill, man.

Dude, you're upset, and you're— —dude, be CAREFUL!

ORE: It's my gun. It's my gun! I don't want to put it down. I want to do this. Let me do it. I want to do it. I want to shoot this gun! It'll be good!

ORE: I don't know what to do with all of this—!

LAD: Well, don't shoot yourself!

ORE: Okay.

LAD: I'm sorry about your dad.

ORE: Punch me in the face.

LAD: What?

ORE: Punch me in the face.

LAD: Put the gun down and I'll punch you in the face.

(ORE *puts the gun down.*)

LAD: Over there somewhere.

(ORE *obliges.*)

ORE: Now punch me in the face.

LAD: No.

(ORE *slaps* LAD *across the face.*)

LAD: Uh. What the fuck?

(ORE *slaps him again. He tries to slap him a third time, but* LAD *blocks him.* ORE *pushes him.*)

LAD: Dude! Chill the fuck out.

(ORE *pushes him.* LAD *pushes him back.*)

ORE: Yes. Yes.
(He pushes him.)
Come on.

(LAD turns to go, but ORE jumps on his back, pulls him to the ground. He punches at him with varying success. LAD, angry now, fights back and lands a solid punch on ORE.)

ORE: More!

(LAD punches ORE again.)

ORE: Thank you!

(LAD wriggles the gun from ORE's grasp, hits him in the face with the butt of it.)

ORE: Ow! Oh god.
(Cries)
Dad!

LAD: Fuck: you okay?

(ORE hits LAD upside the head with the gun. ORE straddles LAD, shoves the gun into his face.)

LAD: You're not thinking.

ORE: If I'm not thinking then what's all this stuff going through my head?

LAD: Dude: there'll be an opportunity to kill people, it'll. Fuckin' present itself, I don't know. The bad guys—kill the bad guys.

ORE: They didn't do anything to me.

LAD: And I did? I'm your friend!

ORE: I'm alone.

LAD: That's not true.

ORE: It's so / fuckin' true.

LAD: You got your sister. You got your.

ORE: Who, my mom? My fucking mom, she, she killed / him...

LAD: So what? You think that makes her not your fucking mom?

ORE: Yeah, that makes her not my fucking mom.

LAD: Okay. Okay!

That makes her the fucking person who murdered my dad.

You're scaring me!

ORE: *(Jamming the gun at LAD)* That takes FUCKING PRECEDENCE!

LAD: Then kill your mom, don't kill me!

(...)

ORE: What did you say?

LAD: Kill your mom! Fuckin'. Fuck!

(...)

ORE: Do people do that?!

LAD: Sure!

ORE: People do that!

LAD: I think so!

ORE: I don't want to be the only person to have done that!

LAD: You aren't!

ORE: Say it again.

LAD: Kill your mom.

ORE: She's the bad guy.

LAD: She's the bad guy.

ORE: I. Mom. I. Huh.

(ORE climbs off of him. LAD rolls over onto his stomach.)

ORE: How do I kill her? I'm here; she's there.

LAD: You could hire someone.

ORE: I'm fuckin' broke. And where am I gonna find a fuckin' hit man, dude?

LAD: I don't know. Someone here must know someone.

ORE: Ha.

LAD: Online?

ORE: That's no fun. Some stranger?

LAD: Your sister could do it.

ORE: My sister? What's she gonna do, do her make up to death? No. No. This is man's work.

LAD: Mother-killing.

ORE: Yeah.

LAD: Fuck.

ORE: If anyone's gonna kill my mom it's gonna be me.

LAD: *(Shivering)* Ooooh! I just got a chill straight / up my…

ORE: I'm gonna kill my / mom.

LAD: *(Shivering again)* Ahhh! There goes another one!

ORE: *(Jumping in place, psyching himself up)* I'm gonna kill her.

LAD: Yeah?

ORE: *(Raising his gun)* Hey, Mom. What's up?

LAD: Gah! *(Kneels, buries his face in the sand, twists from cheek to cheek)* OhmygodIfuckingloveit.

ORE: I gotta get out of here. You'll come with me?

LAD: Really? Yeah. I'll come with.

ORE: *(Aiming his gun at his foot)*

Now I'm gonna blow my fucking foot off. *(…)* This is gonna hurt. Gimme your hand, man.

(LAD *takes his hand.*)

ORE: I'm scared.

LAD: Don't be scared. Think about not here. Air conditioning.

ORE: Movies.

LAD: A bed.

ORE: Good food.

LAD: Rain.

ORE: Snow.

LAD: Pot.

ORE: The pool.

LAD: Water.

ORE: No more sand.

LAD: No more sand. (*…*) You gonna do it?

ORE: Yeah. Just give me a.

(*…*)

LAD: Wait. I have a better idea.

ORE: What?

LAD: Kiss me.

ORE: What did you say?

LAD: Kiss me.

(ORE *wrenches his hand from* LAD*'s.*)

LAD: Hey!

ORE: Are you a fag?

LAD: No. Are you?

ORE: You're a fag.

LAD: I've got a girl back home.

ORE: Fag.

LAD: That's more than you / can say.

ORE: Say you love pussy.

LAD: I love pussy.

ORE: I don't believe you. Where's the clit?

LAD: In and up.

ORE: You don't know.

LAD: Fuck you, you don't know either.

ORE: Fag.

LAD: Dude, hear me out! You shoot yourself in the foot, they'll just put a fuckin' Band-Aid on it and send you right back out.

ORE: What about my knee? My leg: get it amputated?

LAD: How effective is your vengeance gonna be if you're hoppin' around on one leg?

ORE: Huh.

LAD: Remember that guy they discharged last month?

ORE: Yeah.

LAD: They found a picture of him and some other dude at the beach, sharing an ice cream cone, not ice cream though, like gelato or something, and... (*Snaps his fingers*) ...like that. Gone. We could take a picture. A couple of pictures. (*Goes to the laptop, opens it*) Better: a video. Post that shit. Done and done. And keep our fuckin' feet.

ORE: (*Frat boy*) You want me to fuck you?

LAD: What?

ORE: (*"Gentleman"*) Sorry: you want me to make love to you?

LAD: I didn't say anything about that. That's all you, man.

ORE: Please. You're, like, in love with me.

(LAD *types a bit, gets the laptop ready.*)

LAD: It's either this or blow your fuckin' foot off, man. You pick.

(ORE *kneels next to* LAD. LAD *angles the laptop up, aiming the webcam at their faces.*)

ORE: Hey, that's us. Thank god you look gay or no one'd believe it.

LAD: You ready?

ORE: Who goes first?

LAD: I don't care.

ORE: Well, I'm the guy and you're the girl, so.

LAD: Why am / I the—?

ORE: You're the girl.

LAD: Fine, I'm the girl. Whatever. That means you go first.

ORE: So it does. (*He angles his head a little, starts to lean in, pulls away.*) Stop looking at me.

LAD: What, I'm being the girl. Girls look.

ORE: Fuck.

LAD: Sorry. You gonna do it?

ORE: Yeah, just gimme a sec. Whoo. (*He slaps* LAD *across the cheek once with each hand, then darts in and kisses him, quickly, on the mouth. Pulls back.*) Hooah!

LAD: Um.

ORE: What?

LAD: I don't know. Do it again.

(ORE *kisses* LAD. *Pulls back.*)

LAD: Okay…

ORE: What, was that. Like, bad?

LAD: It was fast.

ORE: Well, how long we gotta do it?

LAD: Like a minute. Two minutes.

ORE: Two minutes?!

LAD: It's gotta look real.

ORE: Two minutes and that's fuckin' it.

LAD: I'm gonna put some music on. What's the gayest song you got on here?

ORE: You'll be fuckin' hard-pressed.

LAD: *(Browsing)* No. No. / No.

ORE: That's right.

(LAD clicks a button. John Mayer's Your Body is a Wonderland *begins to play.)*

LAD: Jackpot.

ORE: Someone made me a mix C D!

LAD: You should say something nice to me at the beginning.

ORE: Like what?

LAD: Like tell me I look nice or something.

ORE: You look like fuckin' hell.

LAD: Fuck you, man, don't you know when you're in love with someone they, like, always look nice?

ORE: Shut up. You think I've never been in love with someone before? I know how it goes.

LAD: All right. *(He clicks a button on the laptop.)*

ORE: Is it recording?

LAD: Yep.

(LAD and ORE stare at each other. LAD closes his eyes. ORE leans in and kisses LAD. ORE starts to laugh mid-kiss, pulls away.)

LAD: *(Standing, leaving)* Forget it. Not man enough to just do it, / fake it even.

ORE: What did you just say? I'm not / man enough?

LAD: I thought you were serious about / getting out of here, but no.

ORE: Oh, I'm man enough. You think I won't kiss you? I'm gonna fuckin' kiss you. I'm gonna kiss you so good you'll write in your little fuckin' diary about it.

LAD: Fuck you, man.

ORE: I'm gonna make you wish for ovaries. Get over here, you little bitch.

(LAD sits next to him. ORE leans in and kisses him, for real.)

ORE: How's that?

LAD: Say something nice.

(They kiss again. ORE pulls away, holds LAD's face.)

ORE: I feel. Um. I feel, um. I.

(LAD slaps ORE.)

ORE: I feel safe with you.

(LAD grabs him and kisses him passionately. ORE starts to cry.)

ORE: Oh god. Okay. *(He wipes at his tears.)* Fuck.

LAD: Don't.

(LAD grabs ORE's face, forces his gaze.)

LAD: You're gonna kill her. You're gonna make it right.

ORE: *(Crying)* I will?

LAD: It'll feel good. It'll feel better.

ORE: Okay. (*He shoves* LAD's *hands away, knocks him onto his back, straddles him. Turns back, angles the computer better towards them. Into the camera*) This is for you, Dad.

(*He swoops down, kisses* LAD, *whose body convulses.*)

(*YouTube comments*)

A: woah!. That was HOTT+

B: YOUR GAY

C: fag fuck face deuce

D: soldiers man—what is this opposite day?

E: Sooooooo Cute!…Sorry i lost control. lol

F: I want a kiss like that, haha

G: Do it again!

H: Ask a guy to eat a jelly donut and if he licks his lips and giggles, he's gay.

I: typin w one hadn :)

J: That is not what gay guys act like. Masculine gay guys are not real!

K: time 4 a hate crime

L: YOUR SICK

M: lesbian

N: send em to the front lines

O: OF COURSE YOU'D AUTO ASSUME I'M A LESBIAN. FOR YOUR INFORMATION I AM A STRAIGHT WOMAN (NEVER FELT ATTRACTED TO A WOMAN,, THAT'S JUST ME) AND I JUST DON'T LIKE PEOPLE INSULTING OTHER PEOPLE FOR A STUPID REASON. I DON'T HAVE TO BE SOMETHING TO DEFEND IT. BESIDES IF YOU HATE GAYS SO MUCH, WHY THE HELL DID YOU SAW THIS VIDEO? IS YOUR LIFE THAT BORING? GLAD I'M NOT YOU.

P: aaaaaaaah aaaaaaaaah aaaaaaaaaah

Q: Fuck all you guys who think homo is bad—I'm
sure you'd think differently if it was two girls kissing
;) According to scientists and common knowledge,
people who hate gay people are gay. So straight guys
go jerk off to Angelina Joley and let us women enjoy
this

R: men kissing men = HOT
women kissing women = NOT

Scene Seven

(ELLE's *bedroom*)

(ELLE *sits on her bed with her laptop, watching* ORE *and*
LAD's *video. We hear "Your Body is a Wonderland" from
the computer.*)

ELLE: What the fuck?!

JUSTIN TIMBERLAKE: They're really going.

JUDE LAW: Oh, my.

JUSTIN TIMBERLAKE: That's your brother?

ELLE: *(Shutting off the video)*

Well yeah. But he's usually not. Gay.

ZAC EFRON: No! I—

JUSTIN TIMBERLAKE: You want to watch some more?

ZAC EFRON: Well—maybe they said something at the
end. A code.

JUDE LAW: Honestly: a code?

ZAC EFRON: We could've seen how it played out.

ELLE: There was a code.

JUSTIN TIMBERLAKE: There was?

ELLE: Uh huh. And it said fuck you. *(Eyes full of tears)*
It said fuck you, I don't care, I'm loved and you're not,
you're on your own. *(To her computer)* Well, fuck you
too. *(She slams her laptop shut and gets up from her bed.)*

JUSTIN TIMBERLAKE: Elle.

ZAC EFRON: Elle.

JUDE LAW: Elle.

ZAC EFRON: Don't go.

ELLE: I have nothing.

ZAC EFRON: You have us!

(ELLE stops, turns to them.)

ELLE: What a stupid thing to.

*(ELLE turns, leaves her room, and as she walks outside to the
pool ...)*

JUSTIN TIMBERLAKE: Poor Elle.

ZAC EFRON: Sad Elle.

JUDE LAW: Lonely Elle. You grieve,

ZAC EFRON: and yet

JUSTIN TIMBERLAKE: all we can do

JUDE LAW, JUSTIN TIMBERLAKE, ZAC EFRON: is watch.

*(ELLE stands at the edge of the pool, holding her laptop,
recording one last video.)*

ELLE: One last video. Oh, this hurts, this. *(Sobs)* Where
do you live, where do you—? It doesn't matter, I'm
just, I am. So jealous of you, that you get to, get to
turn your computer off and be with people who love
you and know you and. Cook dinner and. Watch TV
and. Ask you about you and. *(...)* I don't know what
I thought would. Happen, I just. I thought you would
hear me, but you didn't. Who knows if you'll hear this.
I don't know what I believe in anymore. Have fun with

my mom and my brother and the people they love. This is my last video. It's been hell. Goodbye. *(She clicks a button, uploads the video. She lifts her laptop, ready to drop it into the pool. She stops, lowers the laptop, stares at the pool.)* What the…?

(The pool glows with light. Music. At the other end of the pool, BUDDY COX *pulls himself out of the water, fresh from a swim. He wipes the water from his face and hair, looks at* ELLE.*)*

ELLE: Oh my god. You look just like.

BUDDY COX: Hand me a towel?

*(*ELLE *hands* BUDDY COX *a towel from a pool chair.)*

BUDDY COX: Water's great. I hope you weren't planning on dropping that laptop in. Would've blown it entirely.

ELLE: Blown what?

BUDDY COX: Your chance.

ELLE: My chance? Who are you?

BUDDY COX: *(Extending a hand)* Buddy Cox. I'm in television.

OFFSTAGE WHISPERS: Television…
Television…
Television…

BUDDY COX: It's nice to meet you, Elle.

(Blackout)

END OF ACT ONE

ACT TWO

(YouTube video)

THUS: Hey. Um. Since I'm the man of the house, I thought it best if I share some of my fatherly wisdom I've got stored up inside me. I don't have a son—not yet! —I've got a fuckin' nasty-ass daughter, so this won't apply, but this'll be what I tell my son. When he's sitting on my knee. With a fuckin' little—baseball glove. *(He positions the camera. Clears his throat.)*

Son: ladies like you to touch their boobs as if they might break, unless they're married or you're in an elevator. Then they want you to break them.

If you're funny, it's because at some point in time someone didn't want to fuck you.

If a lady's dad has trains, coins, or guns, go into the basement with him and let him show you.

If something itches, don't scratch it.

If something hurts, don't tell anyone.

Don't pay for dinner. Split it. Or better yet, ask if you can borrow some money, can she spot you.

In school you can skip math because nothing ever adds up, science because everything's our fault, and history because it'll all happen again pretty soon. Take shop, though, so you can turn your house into a fort.

Scene One

(The pool)

*(*BUDDY COX, *now in a full suit, sits on a pool chair, talking on his phone.* ELLE *is setting a tray down with two glasses and a pitcher of lemonade on it.)*

BUDDY COX: Uh huh. Uh huh. Uh huh.

*(*ELLE *pours each of them a glass of lemonade.)*

BUDDY COX: Shred it. Shred it. Burn it.

*(*ELLE *hands him a glass of lemonade.)*

BUDDY COX: What else. Uh huh. Accident. What else.

ELLE: Do you want—?

*(*BUDDY COX *holds up a finger to* ELLE: *"One sec.)*

BUDDY COX: What else—I'm with a client.

*(*ELLE *turns away, beaming, mouths: "A client!")*

BUDDY COX: Uh huh. Dressing on the side. Uh huh. Uh huh. Pull the plug. We done? Great. You and your overbite are fired. Gnaw your way out of my office. *(He hangs up the phone with flourish, takes a sip of the lemonade.)*

ELLE: Wow.

BUDDY COX: Delicious lemonade.

ELLE: Thank / you.

BUDDY COX: Fresh-squeezed?

ELLE: I. / What?

BUDDY COX: Keep up, kid. Fresh-squeezed?

ELLE: It's from a / mix, I think.

BUDDY COX: Freaking delicious. Love fresh-squeezed.

*(*BUDDY COX *finishes the lemonade, slowly.* ELLE *can hardly stand still.)*

BUDDY COX: Speaking of fresh squeezes. Let's talk about you.

ELLE: Me?

BUDDY COX: You.

OFFSTAGE WHISPERS: You...

BUDDY COX: That pouty little mouth.

ELLE: What?

BUDDY COX: *(Frames her face with his hands)* Sad. Sad. / Sad.

ELLE: I don't / know what...

BUDDY COX: Your daddy's dead. Come on.

ELLE: Oh. Oh.

BUDDY COX: Grieve.

ELLE: Oh!

BUDDY COX: Good. *(Typing on his Blackberry)* Am I the first one here?

ELLE:...Who?

BUDDY COX: Any of the others been here?

ELLE: The.../ others?

BUDDY COX: Networks.

ELLE: No. Who?

BUDDY COX: *(Checking the pool)* We've seen your videos.

ELLE: You saw my videos? You liked them?

BUDDY COX: We're intrigued.

ELLE: Oh my god: am I going to be on television?

BUDDY COX: Talking about it. Reality show, maybe.

ELLE: Oh my god! Are you for real?

BUDDY COX: Almost insulted by / that question.

ELLE: Me?! On television! AHHHHH!

BUDDY COX: *(Snaps)* Hey. Cut that out.

ELLE: I'm sorry.

BUDDY COX: Sit.

(ELLE *does.* BUDDY COX *reaches in his bag, tosses her a Fruit By The Foot. She eats it.)*

BUDDY COX: *(On the Blackberry)* Your output as of late has been disappointing.

ELLE: I know.

BUDDY COX: Cooling off fast, kid. The last comment was posted twelve hours ago.

ELLE: What am I supposed to do? No one cares about me!

BUDDY COX: Why should they? You're whiny. You're defensive.

ELLE: I know, but it's just—everyone loved me and then everyone loved her, and / I was surprised…

BUDDY COX: So take it back.

ELLE: How?

BUDDY COX: Time for new content.

ELLE: I have some poems I could read.

BUDDY COX: *(Buzzer noise)* Ehhhh. Go further.

ELLE: Please. Tell me what to do and I'll do it. I need to get away from here. You have no idea how much I need this, how much / I've dreamt about this…

BUDDY COX: What brought them to you? Blood, not poems. Blood dries fast. Make more.

ELLE: I'll go far. I will.

BUDDY COX: Good.

ELLE: I'll do anything.

BUDDY COX: *(Looking up from his Blackberry)* Good.

ELLE: Did you see my brother's video?

BUDDY COX: *(Typing again)* Yep.

ELLE: Is he going to be on television?

BUDDY COX: *(Laugh)* No.

ELLE: Good. Is my mom gonna be on it?

BUDDY COX: Yep.

ELLE: Oh. Really? It can't just be me?

BUDDY COX: *(Annoyed, looking up)* She's in at the beginning. Not negotiable. But how long she stays on the show is up to you.

ELLE: Well, I don't see how it could be up to me. She's, like, my mom, I can't get rid of her.

BUDDY COX: You can't?

(ELLE looks at BUDDY COX, whose head is bowed again at his Blackberry.)

ELLE: *(Attempting a joke)* I'd have to...

(ELLE stops. BUDDY COX looks up.)

ELLE: I'd have to.

(...)

OFFSTAGE WHISPERS: Yes?

ELLE: Oh.

(BUDDY COX frames ELLE's face once more.)

BUDDY COX: Smile.

Scene Two

(An airport gate waiting area)

(ORE and LAD sit, in civilian clothes. PATRICE is next to them. ORE fidgets, pokes at LAD.)

LAD: Will you sit still, man?

ORE: I can't.

LAD: Read the fuckin' magazine.

ORE: No.

LAD: Do the crossword.

ORE: No, they make me feel stupid.

LAD: Then go to sleep.

ORE: I can't.

LAD: You want a pill?

ORE: Yeah, give me a pill.

(ORE swallows the pill, gulps at the drink, appeased. LAD makes eye contact with PATRICE, who smiles at them.)

PATRICE: *(Deep South)* Where are you boys from?

ORE: *(Under his breath)* Great.

LAD: Omaha. He's from Greenwich.

PATRICE: Oh! How nice. This a homecoming trip?

ORE: Yeah.

LAD: Don't mumble, man.

ORE: YEAH.

LAD: *(To PATRICE)* His mom and his sister are there. Goin' for a visit.

PATRICE: Are you?

LAD: Yup.

PATRICE: Tee hee. Tee hee hee. I'm sorry. I just.

(PATRICE *has a laughing fit.* LAD *and* ORE *exchange a look.*)

PATRICE: It's just that I. Hee. I know who you are. I was gonna pretend I didn't, but I just. I just couldn't keep it together.

ORE: What?

LAD: She knows us!

ORE: How?

PATRICE: I'm so excited. I've seen all of your family's videos—your mom's, your sister's. We watch 'em in my quilt group. I had to close my eyes during yours, no offense, I can't even watch Tom Hanks and Meg Ryan kiss, I just, that's just me, that's my lot, I'm shut off from my body. Could I ask you to sign my boarding pass?

(PATRICE *hands it to* LAD, *along with a pen.*)

LAD: Um, sure.

ORE: She saw our video? People are seeing it?

PATRICE: My husband Paul... (*Shouting over their seats*) Paul! (*To* LAD *and* ORE) My husband will be so excited... (*Shouting again*) Paul!

PAUL: (*From behind them*) What?

PATRICE: Get over here!

PAUL: What is it, woman?

PATRICE: Look at who I'm sitting next to! (*To* LAD *and* ORE) Ever since I started watchin' your mom's videos he won't let me out of his sight. He insists on sitting behind me, walkin' behind me—he sleeps in our son's old room with the door locked. He doesn't want me gettin' any ideas.

PAUL: Woman's unhinged.

PATRICE: *(Cheery)* Keep it up, Paul! I'm an ideas woman! *(To* ORE *and* LAD*)* So what's on the agenda for when y'all get home?

LAD: I'm gonna meet everybody, / meet his mom, and.

PATRICE: Lovely.

PAUL: You gonna kill her?

LAD: Yeah. Well, he is.

PAUL: *(To* ORE*)* Good on ya, sir.

PATRICE: Oh my heavens. You are?

PAUL: Yessiree, look at 'em. They're men on a mission.

PATRICE: *(Hand to her heart, eyes teary)* I suppose this was inevitable. All these stories end this way.

PAUL: She upset the natural order / of things!

PATRICE: Paul, I don't want to hear another one / of your rants.

LAD: She killed his dad!

PATRICE: Oh, this is horrible. *(To* ORE*)* How can you? She's your momma. You're here because of her.

LAD: Okay, that's enough. / Please leave us alone.

PAUL: Aw, they don't wanna hear none of your / bleedin'-heart claptrap, Patrice, they want blood.

PATRICE: Oh, Paul, / for heaven's sake.	LAD: *(To* ORE*)* Come on, let's move. We don't / board for another half hour.
PAUL: There's a war on, Patrice.	ORE: Wait, I.
PATRICE: Hers was not the first stone cast!	LAD: What is it?

PAUL: I never should've let you start takin' those night classes. An / old lady in with the young people.

PATRICE: Let me! I went of my own / accord!

PAUL: Noise, noise, noise.

LAD: Don't listen to them.

ORE: I'm.

LAD: What?

ORE: I don't know.

PATRICE: I will kill you, Paul Stokely.

PAUL: Then Bobby'll come and kill you, avenge his daddy.

PATRICE: Let him! I'm goin' to heaven. I'm goin' with my / Lord and

Savior Jesus Christ.

PAUL: You're goin' to hell, woman.

PATRICE: No, you are. You're meetin' your maker. Satan made you!

ORE: I didn't know people. Knew, I don't. I don't want people knowing, I don't want people to look at me and know.

| LAD: Okay, okay... just take a deep breath and... | ORE: They know and they don't think I'm right. Everybody's looking at me. |
| Nobody's looking at you. It's just me. I'm looking at you. I know you. Only me. | Everybody knows me, knows what I'm doing. |

PATRICE: Soon as that plane lands back home I'm killin' you. We'll eat in the airport, get you your last meal, and then it's lights out.

PAUL: *(Standing)* SHE SAID BOMB! SHE SAID BOMB!

(PATRICE stands, hits him upside the head. He grabs her and chokes her.)

(LAD *reaches up and covers* ORE's *ears. The brawl sounds cut out. Silence.*)

OFFSTAGE WHISPERS: Sssshhhh…

LAD: You are just. You are just. You are ju—

(ORE *kisses* LAD.)

Scene Three

(The backyard. Day)

(CLYT *is sitting in a pool chair.* THUS *films her with a camera on a tripod.*)

CLYT: I don't know quite what to say, Janelle from Dallas. Every marriage is different, and different solutions work for different people. Who's to say that what worked in my marriage would work in yours? I'm no expert. Oh, Janelle, I feel for you. I really do.

THUS: *(Reading from index cards)* YLFR238 asks, "What's your favorite color?"

CLYT: Navy, offset by white. *(…)* So many of you asked questions, I'm absolutely delighted.

THUS: MikeRunner82 asks, "What kind of music do you listen to?"

CLYT: *(To the camera)* I have to say, Joan Baez, Carole King, Tina Turner: my gals from back in the day! A little "Kanye" for the treadmill. Michael Buble for the car. What kind of music do you like, MikeRunner82? Anything you'd care to recommend?

THUS: BobbyKennedy asks, "What do you look for in a man?"

CLYT: *(To* THUS*)* Thus, darling, come and sit next to me.

(THUS *joins* CLYT *on the pool chair.*)

CLYT: This is what I look for in a man. A confident smile.

(THUS *smiles for the camera.*)

CLYT: Brawn.

(THUS *flexes, kisses a bicep.*)

CLYT: An awareness of politics.

THUS: I quite liked Ron Paul.

CLYT: A romantic spirit.

(THUS *kisses* CLYT *on the cheek.*)

CLYT: And, last but not least, strong paternal instincts.

THUS: *(To an imaginary child)* As long as you live under my roof you're taking piano lessons!

(THUS *nuzzles* CLYT*'s neck.*)

CLYT: You sweet, sweet thing. I've taught you so many things.

(THUS *paws at* CLYT*'s breasts.*)

CLYT: How to get a pool nice and clean. How to poach an egg.

(THUS *buries his face in* CLYT*'s cleavage.*)

CLYT: How to tie a tie. To make meaningful eye contact while greeting someone.

(THUS *looks up at* CLYT.)

THUS: Hello.

CLYT: Hello. Look at you. A woman-made man.

(He kisses her.)

(ELLE approaches from the house, wearing her bathing suit and carrying a bouquet of flowers. BUDDY COX follows behind her, snapping his fingers and ordering a CAMERAMAN around.)

ELLE: Ah-hem.

CLYT: Well, hello, dear! *(...)* What is all this?

ELLE: Oh, don't mind us. We're just filming my new video.

CLYT: I see that. *(Approaching BUDDY COX)* And who is this?

ELLE: Don't bother him; he's / very busy.

BUDDY COX: Buddy Cox.

CLYT: Pleasure.

BUDDY COX: All mine.

ELLE: He's in television.

CLYT: I didn't know we'd attracted the industry! Did you offer our guest some lemonade?

ELLE: He has had lemonade.

CLYT: Ours?

ELLE: Mine.

CLYT: You made your own?

ELLE: It's a fucking mix.

CLYT: I'm impressed, darling. You've learned something from me.

ELLE: You just add water and stir.

CLYT: *(Dead stare on BUDDY COX)* The key is in the wrist. *(...)* We were just finishing up our latest video. A

"Q & A" session with some of the fans. We'll get out of your hair.

ELLE: Actually, I'd like you to stay.

(…)

CLYT: You would?

ELLE: Yes. I want you to watch.

(CLYT turns to THUS.)

CLYT: Well! Isn't this the greatest day!

ELLE: Not him.

THUS: Fuck you!

CLYT: *(To THUS)* Run on in the house, dear. I'll be there shortly. This is just for us girls. Please?

(THUS exits. CLYT sits.)

BUDDY COX: We ready? Got the pool in there?

(The CAMERAMAN nods.)

BUDDY COX: *(Looks up for a moment)* Looks great.

ELLE: I do?

BUDDY COX: *(Back down)* Yep.

ELLE: I feel weird.

(BUDDY COX doesn't look up.)

ELLE: I don't look weird?

CLYT: You look beautiful, dear. Your / hair blown out.

ELLE: Shut up. *(To BUDDY COX)* Shouldn't I be in, I don't know, something more… *(Fusses with the bathing suit)* This feels like I'm a little kid.

BUDDY COX: Young's good.

CLYT: It leaves more to the imagination.

BUDDY COX: *(Putting the phone away)* Let's start.

(ELLE *perks up, glad to have his attention. The*
CAMERAMAN *holds up his hand, counts down: 3, 2, 1.)*

CLYT: Stand up straight, dear.

ELLE: Shut up.

BUDDY COX: Action.

ELLE: *(Memorized)* Daddy…oh, Daddy…why were you
taken from me? *(She tosses a flower into the pool.)* I'd
barely gotten to / know you…

CLYT: Louder, dear.

ELLE: *(Louder)* I'd barely gotten to know you…you, like
all men, are a mystery to me.

(CLYT *gestures for* ELLE *to stand up straight.)*

ELLE: How will I /…how will…

CLYT: *(Whispering)* Graceful. Arch.

ELLE: *(To* BUDDY COX) She won't shut up!

CLYT: I simply would like to see some poise, Mister
Cox. She is not a street urchin, she's a young woman.

ELLE: Mom! This is not your video!

CLYT: Well, that's certainly clear.

BUDDY COX: *(Blackberry out)* You gonna let her talk to
you like that?

ELLE: I. *(To* CLYT, *gesturing to* BUDDY COX) Look what
you did!

CLYT: Don't fret, darling. It was just the first take. You
were nervous.

ELLE: I wasn't / nervous!

CLYT: *(To the* CAMERAMAN) Let's take it from the top,
shall we?

ELLE: Jesus Christ. Buddy?

(BUDDY COX *holds up a finger.)*

CLYT: Turn out, dear. You're holding flowers. Big eyes.

(BUDDY COX *puts his phone away.*)

BUDDY COX: From the top?

CLYT: From the top.

(*The* CAMERAMAN *signals: 3, 2, 1.*)

CLYT: (*Whispered*) Smile!

ELLE: I am not smiling—I am sad. (*She collects herself.*)
Daddy…oh Daddy…why were you taken from me?
(*She tosses a flower into the pool.*) I'd barely gotten to
know you. You, like all men, are a mystery to me. How
will I learn, who will teach me, those things that only a
father could teach?

(CLYT *turns to the* CAMERAMAN, *points to herself, mouths:*
"Me?")

ELLE: I guess I'll have to learn them myself. (*She tosses
another flower into the pool.*) Because you were taken
from me. Someone murdered you.

(CLYT *turns to the* CAMERAMAN, *mouths:* "Me".)

ELLE: You're buried out here in the backyard without
so much as a proper tombstone or coffin, just your
body in the ground. You didn't have a funeral. No one
said kind words over your body. No one brought you
flowers. Except for me.

(ELLE *goes to the stereo, presses a button. Sarah
McLachlan's* Angel *begins to play.*)

ELLE: I'm no longer a girl… (*She tosses a flower.*) …
but I'm not yet a woman… (*She tosses another flower.*)
Everything / is so confusing…

CLYT: Oh, dear, this is. Did you write this?

ELLE: What?

CLYT: Are these your words?

(BUDDY COX *signals for the* CAMERAMAN *to get* CLYT, *too.)*

ELLE: Yes! / Why?

CLYT: No longer a / girl, not yet a woman…

ELLE: Yeah, what's the problem? It's true!

CLYT: Quite frankly, dear, you are going to be attracting a certain kind of attention, / talking like that.

ELLE: I want to attract attention, / I want people.

CLYT: The wrong kind of / attention, if you ask me.

ELLE: I don't want to leave stuff to the imagination, I don't want people to imagine me, I want people to have me.

CLYT: Oh, they'll have you all right.

(ELLE *goes to the stereo, starts the song over.)*

ELLE: *(To the* CAMERAMAN*)* I'm starting again. I'm going to need more flowers soon. *(…)* I'm no longer a girl. *(Tosses a flower)* I'm not / yet a woman.

CLYT: Well, I've / seen enough.

ELLE: *(To* CLYT*)* Oh, you are such bullshit, you / know that, right?

CLYT: I beg your pardon!

ELLE: Stop acting like you're some fucking lady warrior, some champion and protector of women. You're bullshit.

CLYT: Well! I haven't had such a sophisticated analysis of my character in / quite some time…

ELLE: If you actually thought women could do stuff you'd be scared of me.

CLYT: You?

ELLE: Yes!

CLYT: Why should I be afraid of you? My / little girl?

ELLE: Unbelievable. You're bullshit.

CLYT: And you, dear, are making a mess in my pool. Please clean all of this up when you are done. *(To the others)* Well, this all feels very silly and I doubt that my participation is needed beyond this—

(ELLE tosses her props to the side, lunges at CLYT, tackles her to the ground, choking her.)

ELLE: I'll kill you! I'll kill you! You bitch, I'll kill you!	CLYT: Elle! What are you—? Help me!

(The CAMERAMAN moves to break up the fight, but BUDDY COX stops him.)

BUDDY COX: *(To the CAMERAMAN)* Not your job. Do your job.

(BUDDY COX moves in, yanks ELLE to her feet, holds her back. CLYT rolls over, gasping.)

ELLE: *(Raging)* I will! I'll do it!

BUDDY COX: You will. Not yet.

ELLE: Let me do it! I had my hands around her, I really felt like I could do it.

BUDDY COX: This is the teaser. Save some for the show.

CLYT: *(Still on the ground)* The show?

ELLE: Yes, yes, the show, my show, it's a show about me, about me killing you. No one else will do it, so I'll do it myself! *(…)* Oh, sweet, listen to this: you're quiet. Haven't heard this in fucking ages. Oh, fuck, I forgot the. What's the. Line? *(To BUDDY COX)* How was that? Was that right?

BUDDY COX: So, so, so right.

(YouTube comments)

A: Goodbye bitch

B: Y R U so angry???

C: AWESOME THERE YOU ARE

D: Got chills

E: LOLOLOLOL you are CRAZY and I love it. Are you ever in Fort Lauderdale? You should come and visit. I know the best places to go.

F: its mothers d-day

G: shit she looked scared

H: look at those lips man lips lips lips liiiiiiiiiiiiiick

I: Just another day in the JEWNITED STATES OF AMERICA

J: YOU'VE COME A LONG WAY BABY

K: i'll teach her about man things—i've got the biggest lesson right here

L: V. V. V. Voooooooom

M: Too much talking not enough sucking

N: maybe i can do them both and settle this fare and square

O: Great, the JEW-S-A troll is back.

P: sluuuuuuuuuuuuuuuuuuuuuuuuuuuuurp

Q: You all are pigs. She lost her dad and all you can do is talk about her lips.

R: I'd like to see you try & fight me

S: god could this girl whine any more??? thanks 4 setting our gender back decades, stupid bitch

T: Kill Kill Kill

U: This just got good again!

V: not true—i'd love to cumfort her—get it? cum fort

Scene Four

(ELLE's *bedroom.*)

(ELLE *sits at her computer, still in her bathing suit from earlier in the day.*)

ZAC EFRON: Elle?

JUDE LAW: Elle?

JUSTIN TIMBERLAKE: Elle.

(…)

JUDE LAW: Elle.

JUSTIN TIMBERLAKE: Elle.

ZAC EFRON: Elle. (…) Elle!

JUSTIN TIMBERLAKE: Elle!

JUDE LAW: Elle!

ELLE: Oh my god, these comments are…insane. These guys want to have sex with me. What do you think they look like? Do you think they're, like, fat and old, or do you think they're hot?

JUDE LAW: You do not know these people.

JUSTIN TIMBERLAKE: They're words.

ELLE: So what? You're pieces of paper taped to my wall. At least these words are coming from actual people.

ZAC EFRON: We're pictures of actual people!

ELLE: I bought you at the mall.

ZAC EFRON: God! (*He cries.*)

ELLE: Um, this was all your idea. Remember?

JUSTIN TIMBERLAKE: We were wrong.

JUDE LAW: We have been deceived.

ELLE: (*Scoffing*) Deceived?

JUDE LAW: We hoped they would be of comfort to you.

JUSTIN TIMBERLAKE: The public has helped us.

ZAC EFRON: Saved us.

JUSTIN TIMBERLAKE: Lifted us out of tragedy.

JUDE LAW: Ah, but things,

ZAC EFRON: the times,

JUDE LAW: the people have changed.

JUSTIN TIMBERLAKE: I used to be able to open a letter from a fan,

JUDE LAW: and it would say,

ZAC EFRON: I love you.

JUSTIN TIMBERLAKE: I'm sorry for your loss.

JUDE LAW: I wish you nothing

JUSTIN TIMBERLAKE: but the

ZAC EFRON: best.

ELLE: Well, fine. These aren't letters, but they're still wishing me the best, I think.

ZAC EFRON: No.

JUSTIN TIMBERLAKE: No.

JUDE LAW: No.

ELLE: It's still the public!

JUDE LAW: These

ZAC EFRON: These

JUSTIN TIMBERLAKE: These

JUDE LAW: These are rapists.

ELLE: I don't know what you want me to do. I listened to you. I did what you told me to do. And now you're saying this? Come on.

JUSTIN TIMBERLAKE: We didn't want you to lose sight of yourself.

ELLE: Maybe I'm actually seeing myself for the first time. I can't even get a guy to look at me at school, and these guys are talking about my lips and my boobs and—and my body, which I've always hated, and. I mean, I know you talk about taking care of me, but do you, like, want me?

JUSTIN TIMBERLAKE: Sure!

JUDE LAW: Of course we do.

ELLE: You want to have sex with me?

JUDE LAW: After a proper courtship!

ELLE: God, you guys treat me like a delicate little flower.

JUDE LAW: *(Sharp)* All right.

JUSTIN TIMBERLAKE: *(Sharp)* All right.

ZAC EFRON: *(Sharp)* All right.

JUDE LAW: Grown up talk, then. How will you kill your mother?

ELLE: I don't know.

JUDE LAW: You don't think you should have some sort of plan?

ELLE: It'll come to me.

JUSTIN TIMBERLAKE: You should probably think that through.

ELLE: Look, what matters right now is that people are watching me again and not her. So I don't know right now, okay, but I'll know later. Shit, I can even ask them. *(She turns on her camera, talks into it.)* Hey bitches, it's me, Elle. I'm taking a poll: how should I kill my mom? Use my daddy's gun? Stab her with her carving knife? I don't know. I'm open to your ideas. Also:

should this be a two-piece? I'm feeling stifled. My body wants out. What do you think? *(She finishes the video, uploads it.)* Now we just sit here and wait. God, it's like Christmas and I'm at the. Top of the stairs.
(Clicks a button) Six people have watched it already— oh my god. Awesome. *(Clicks a button)* Twelve. *(Clicks a button)* Come on. *(Clicks a button)* Here we go. *(Reads)* "kill her with what hot yung bod." *(Turns the posters, defiant)* Hmm! *(Clicks a button)* "KNIFE DEF TWO PIECE DEF DO IT ALL" *(Clicks a button)* "u can use my gun it's already loaded and ready for ur use" *(Clicks a button)* "How about / no piece? Let..."

JUSTIN TIMBERLAKE: *(Voice of comments comes from his mouth)* How about no piece? Let that body out entirely.

ELLE: Maybe I will!

ZAC EFRON: *(Voice of comments)* what about stranguling

ELLE: I'll add that to the list.

JUDE LAW: *(Voice of comments)* r u gonna show us ur tits & u killing ur mom

ELLE: We'll see!

JUDE LAW: NO COVER THAT SHIT UP

ELLE: Fuck off, loser!

JUSTIN TIMBERLAKE: Hi, Elle, it's me, Howard, and I just wanted to see if you'd watched / my video yet...

ELLE: Oh my god. Refresh.

JUDE LAW: *¡Usted es hermoso!*

ELLE: *De nada.*

ZAC EFRON: forget ur mom just come live with me you won't have to kill me only kiss me

JUDE LAW: Where do you stay at?

JUSTIN TIMBERLAKE: Gun. Two piece.

ZAC EFRON: go suicide—make the world better

ELLE: Um, you go suicide.

JUDE LAW: Use MY DICK to kill your mom!!!

JUSTIN TIMBERLAKE: OPEN UR MOUTH

(ELLE *clicks*.)

JUDE LAW: spread those legs

(*Clicks*)

ZAC EFRON: feeling lonely?
click here for love

JUDE LAW: click here for love

JUSTIN TIMBERLAKE: click here for my dick

ZAC EFRON: move the camera down—don't need so
much face

JUDE LAW: don't make us beg

JUSTIN TIMBERLAKE: DON'T MAKE US WAIT
ANYMORE.

(ELLE *grabs a pair of scissors and begins to slice through her
bathing suit, cutting it into a two-piece.*)

JUDE LAW: ill kiss ur neck

JUSTIN TIMBERLAKE: tease ur tit

ZAC EFRON: bite ur hip

JUSTIN TIMBERLAKE: tongue ur slit

ZAC EFRON: make u scream

JUDE LAW: pull ur hair

JUSTIN TIMBERLAKE: make u mine

ZAC EFRON: i'll fuck you so hard you'll scream like ur
bein killed

JUDE LAW: Seriesly stop being such a tease just do it
alreadyt

(ELLE *slams her laptop shut, catches her breath.* BUDDY COX *enters, on his phone. He tosses a knife onto her bed.*)

BUDDY COX: Knife.

ELLE: Did you like it?

BUDDY COX: Was a good one. (*Looks at her bathing suit*) What did you do?

ELLE: They want me in a two-piece.

BUDDY COX: And I want you in one. Fix it.

ELLE: Too late, what's done is done.

BUDDY COX: We'll get you another.

ELLE: Are you married?

BUDDY COX: No.

ELLE: Do you have a girlfriend?

BUDDY COX: No.

ELLE: Boyfriend?

BUDDY COX: No.

ELLE: Oh. Cool. I mean, that's a shame. Big strong man like you.

(BUDDY COX *doesn't look up.*)

ELLE: We've had a serious shortage of your kind around here. Ever since my daddy is murdered.

BUDDY COX: Huh.

(ELLE *reaches out, touches* BUDDY COX*'s crotch. He doesn't look up.*)

BUDDY COX: Fuck are you doing.

ELLE: Hi. (…) Uh, hi. I. (*She kneels in front of him.*) Can I—?

BUDDY COX: Don't love you.

ELLE: That's fine. I don't need that. I've done this a hundred times. *(She struggles to undo the belt buckle on his pants.)*

BUDDY COX: *(Stepping away, still typing on the Blackberry)* I'll pass.

(ELLE covers her face.)

ELLE: *(Mortified)* Okay.

BUDDY COX: Got a thing.

ELLE: Okay. *(Laughs a little, looks away)* Actually, that wasn't true. I haven't even done it once. I'm a virgin.

(BUDDY COX looks up at her, smiles. He puts his Blackberry away.)

Scene Five

(A motel room. Early evening)

(ORE enters. LAD is standing on the bed.)

LAD: *(Frantic)* Did you do it without me?

ORE: No. Why are you / standing…

LAD: You promise?

ORE: *(Sitting on the bed, kicking off his shoes)* Yes. What the / fuck, man.

LAD: *(Sitting next to him, hugging him)* Oh, thank god. I thought you'd—I don't know what I thought—I hoped you wouldn't—you stink, / where have you…

ORE: I need a shower.

LAD: Me too. Let's shower. Do I stink? I was so sweaty and—freaked out—and you left while I was sleeping, what a dick move, dude.

ORE: I'm sorry.

LAD: Oh my god, I'm going out of my skin, just, like, needy, and—where have you been? Listen to me, I might as well be in a dress—but: where have you been?

ORE: I went by the house.

LAD: You did?

ORE: Yeah.

LAD: How'd you—?

ORE: I walked.

LAD: The whole way?

ORE: Yeah.

LAD: What did you do?

ORE: Sat outside. Hid.

LAD: All day?

ORE: Yeah. I watched.

LAD: Oh man, I trained in that, surveillance, I could've—

ORE: You could've what?

LAD: I don't know, brought you snacks.

ORE: The pool boy mowed the lawn. Sprinklers turned on. The mail came. That was all that happened. *(Lies on the bed)* That and I spooked myself out.

LAD: And you didn't do anything?

ORE: No.

LAD: You promise?

ORE: Shut the fuck / up, man.

LAD: Sorry, it's just that time is / of the essence...

ORE: I'm taking my time, making / sure it's right.

LAD: *(Quickly)* All I will say to / that is...

ORE: Jesus.

LAD: A plan. Just a / plan. A plan?

ORE: Friday. Friday. Friday.

LAD: Two days from now.

ORE: It's her birthday. What, you think I'm putting no thought into this?

(…)

LAD: I'm sorry.

ORE: Thank you.

LAD: I'm an idiot. This is pretty much the most exciting thing to ever happen to, well, I feel silly saying to me, but you know—and it's making me crazy, like I'm, this is what happens when you leave for a whole day. Don't do it again. *(Kisses ORE's shoulders)* Include me. Include me. Include me. / Include me. Include me.

ORE: *(Laughing)* Okay. Okay.

LAD: Do you know what I did today? I went to YouTube, into those comments, and I defended you. Told them what you're going to do, told them that when they see you do it they're going to see you how I see you.

ORE: *(Standing)* Going to shower. Want to be included?

LAD: Yes, please. *(Grabbing the laptop)* Film it?

Scene Six

(CLYT's bedroom. Years ago)

(CLYT sits up in bed. Morning sounds. The sun is suddenly bright—too bright.)

(NON enters, sits on the edge of the bed, in a bathing suit with a towel draped around his neck.)

NON: I think building that pool was the best decision we ever made. *(He crosses through to the bathroom, offstage. O S)* Every morning I get up and I geek out over that pool. *(He reappears, the towel now wrapped around his waist.)* It's awesome to wake up and be thrilled by what's to come. How many of us get to say that? *(He cleans his ears with a Q-Tip.)* I go to bed thinking about it, and sometimes I hate having to go to sleep; I want to blink and have it be morning already. *(He applies deodorant under his arms.)* Why don't you get in the pool today? It would do you some good. Might help with the pain. You can hurt less, if that appeals to you. *(He sits on the edge of the bed, clips his toenails.)* There was a deer in the yard this morning. We stared at each other like two fools in this crazy world, and I swear to God he smiled at me, nodded, and I dove into the pool with his blessing. The water is always cold at first, and you think you just might die, like the cold'll freeze your heart, but then you feel warm and you're floating. *(He glances down at his crotch.)* Aaaand now I'm hard. Now I can't proceed. Slave to it. *(He turns to her, opens his towel.)* Blow me, babe? *(…)* Oh, come on. It won't take me long. *(He closes the towel.)* Fine. *(He dresses, puts on a suit.)*

CLYT: I wish upon you everything I am feeling.

NON: Helpful?

CLYT: Why should you have pleasure? I wish you pain. I / wish you suffering.

NON: There are things you can do, you can swim, the water is warm, it will / feel good.

CLYT: I can't bathe. I can't be submerged in water. Did you even listen to what they said. *(Pounds the bed, whimpers)* You deceived me. You told me this was right, but I am in such pain.

NON: It was right. We did it, it's done, no / sense dwelling...

CLYT: You did it.

NON: You did it too.

CLYT: I wanted another.

NON: What would we have done with another?

CLYT: I wanted another. All I wanted was another and now, now I have none.

NON: You have two.

CLYT: You have two; they don't look at me.

NON: Don't act like we didn't think about this.

CLYT: No, no, no.

NON: To raise a child is to constantly be at war. Did you really want to suit up again? I didn't. I'd like to survive a little for once.

CLYT: I gave you my body, my honor, my life. I bled for you. You were supposed to protect me from harm.

NON: I'm sorry.

CLYT: I should have killed you here. (*She makes a gun with her fingers and aims it at him.*)

OFFSTAGE WHISPERS: Bang...

NON: (*Breaking from the scene, agreeing with her*) Yeah, that would've been good. (*Stands, smooths out his tie*) See you soon. (*Kisses her forehead*)

Scene Seven

(ELLE's *bedroom*)

(BUDDY COX *sits on the edge of her bed, tying his shoes and staring intently at an e-mail on his Blackberry.*)

(ELLE *is in the bed next to him, staring at his back.*)

JUDE LAW: *(Softly)* Elle...

ELLE: Oh. You're done?

BUDDY COX: Work.

ELLE: Right.

JUSTIN TIMBERLAKE: *(Softly)* Elle...

ELLE: You don't want to do anything else?

BUDDY COX: No.

ELLE: I thought you might—want to? I mean, we didn't do anything. For me.

BUDDY COX: Rain check.

ELLE: Oh. Okay. Whatever.

ZAC EFRON: *(Softly)* Elle...

(BUDDY COX *goes to the door.*)

ELLE: You're leaving?

BUDDY COX: Busy here.

ELLE: Um, okay?

JUDE LAW: Oh, Elle.

JUSTIN TIMBERLAKE: Oh, Elle.

ZAC EFRON: Oh, Elle.

BUDDY COX: Thanks for that.

ELLE: Was it any good?

BUDDY COX: It was fine.

ELLE: I feel like I didn't do anything. You just, like, used my mouth.

BUDDY COX: Right. That's all we need.

ELLE: But there are, I don't know, things I could do, as me, that might / make it better.

BUDDY COX: It was fine.

ELLE: I want to be good at it.

JUSTIN TIMBERLAKE: You want

ZAC EFRON: and you want

JUDE LAW: and you do not get.

BUDDY COX: This was obviously a mistake.

ELLE: What?

BUDDY COX: Should've known better but virgins are my crack. *(Moving to the door)* Make another video. Bat your eyelashes, play with the knife. Get 'em revved up again. I'll be by tomorrow.

ELLE: Fine! BYE!

BUDDY COX: Don't do that. It's annoying.

ELLE: Will you look at me while you talk?

(BUDDY COX looks up at ELLE.)

ELLE: You just used me.

BUDDY COX: You asked if you could give me a blowjob. I said yes. You gave me a blowjob. Where did we go wrong?

ELLE: That was—that was the first time I'd ever done it! You're my first!

BUDDY COX: What, should I have lit a candle?

ELLE: *(Crying)* That was my first time and you aren't even being nice to me, you're being mean. This is awful. It's not supposed to be like this.

BUDDY COX: *(Framing her face)* We should be filming this.

ELLE: You're a horrible person. Why are you alive and my dad is dead?

BUDDY COX: Hey. He was more like me than you think.

ELLE: Your dick is small.

BUDDY COX: *(Turning to leave)* Yeah, well, you give a shitty blowjob so we're even.

(ELLE picks up the knife from her bed.)

ZAC EFRON: Oh!

JUSTIN TIMBERLAKE: Oh!

JUDE LAW: Oh!

(ELLE stabs BUDDY COX with it.)

JUDE LAW: ELLE!

JUSTIN TIMBERLAKE: ELLE!

ZAC EFRON: ELLE!

(BUDDY COX drops to his knees, dying.)

BUDDY COX: No, wait—I! *(He gets out his Blackberry, drops to his elbows, struggling to type.)* Out. Of. Office. *(He dies.)*

JUSTIN TIMBERLAKE: Elle!

JUDE LAW: Elle!

ZAC EFRON: Elle!

ELLE: SHUT UP! *(She reaches for JUSTIN TIMBERLAKE's picture.)*

JUSTIN TIMBERLAKE: Wait! What are you doing?

(ELLE tears down his picture. His scream echoes, quiets. She reaches for ZAC EFRON's picture.)

ZAC EFRON: This isn't you! You're better than this! You're kind and you're caring and you're silly and when you're hurt you're hurt and you don't…

(ELLE tears down his picture.)

JUDE LAW: If I may, before I go, seeing as how I was the first one up on this wall…

(ELLE pauses.)

JUDE LAW: Decisions are not islands. They are bound to neighboring land. It might have been easy to take a life, but you will find a portion of yours has also been taken. And with that, I go.

(ELLE *tears his picture down, crumples them all and tosses them to the floor. She stands, clutching the torn bathing suit on her body, tries to reattach the sliced ends.*)

Scene Eight

(*The motel room. Very early morning*)

(ORE *is sitting up in bed.* LAD *sleeps next to him.*)

OFFSTAGE WHISPERS: W W W W W W W W W W W...

(ORE *shakes his head, tries to ignore.*)

OFFSTAGE WHISPERS: W W W W W W W W W W W...

(*He picks up the laptop, opens it. The screen illuminates his face in the dark room. He types. Reads.*)

B: YOUR GAY

C : fag fuck face deuce

ORE: Oh, shit, / come on...

D: soldiers man—what is this opposite day?

E: Sooooooo Cute!...Sorry i lost control. lol

F: I want a kiss like that, haha

G: Do it again!

ORE: Wouldn't you / like to see...

H: Ask a guy to eat a jelly donut and if he licks his lips and giggles, he's gay.

I: typin w one hadn :)

J: That is not what gay guys act like. Masculine gay guys are not real!

ORE: Who the fuck / are you, you fat piece of…

K: time 4 a hate crime

L: YOUR SICK

ORE: Jesus, I…

N: send em to the front lines

(ORE *slams the laptop shut.*)

OFFSTAGE WHISPERS: W W W W W W W W W W W W…

ORE: Stop it.

OFFSTAGE WHISPERS: We see you…

ORE: Well, I don't hear you.

OFFSTAGE WHISPERS: Faggot…

ORE: No.

OFFSTAGE WHISPERS: Murderer…

ORE: Oh god.

OFFSTAGE WHISPERS: Faggot…
Murderer…
Girl…
Pussy…
Killer…
Soft…
Cocksucker…
Mother-killer…
Momma's boy…

ORE: Stop! Please!

OFFSTAGE WHISPERS: W W W We see you…

(*Sirens in the distance. They get closer.*)

OFFSTAGE WHISPERS: W W W We are coming…

ORE: I don't understand! I'm scared!

OFFSTAGE WHISPERS: Little boy…

ORE: Yes! I am!

OFFSTAGE WHISPERS: Soon…

ORE: Yes?

OFFSTAGE WHISPERS: Soon you will be our son…

(The door swings open and NON *backs into the room, kissing a* YOUNG WOMAN. *They are very drunk. They're laughing.* ORE *leaps from the bed.)*

ORE: Dad?

*(*NON *turns around, lets go of the* YOUNG WOMAN. ORE*'s face goes white. He drops to his knees.)*

NON: Huh. That's funny. *(Looks at the key in his hand)* They must've given us the same room.

ORE: It's you.

NON: You look like shit, son.

ORE: Can't sleep. You're dead.

NON: And what, you're sad?

ORE: Yes, I'm sad.

NON: Huh. Warms an old man's heart. Didn't think you liked me that much.

ORE: I didn't. Who is she?

NON: Let me tell you: Hell is lousy with easy lays. You almost done with the bed? We kinda need it.

ORE: Get your own room. This is mine.

NON: You want a go at her first? You look like you could use it.

ORE: No thanks.

NON: Wait a second.

ORE: What?

NON: It looks like you've already got someone / in your bed…

ORE: No. No, Dad, wait…

(NON *goes to the bed, tears off the covers to reveal* LAD *sleeping. He looks up at* ORE. ORE *sits in the bed, almost protective.* NON *goes to the closet.*)

NON: Where's your uniform?

ORE: Don't have it. They took it. I got kicked out.

NON: Are you planning on avenging me?

ORE: Planning on it.

NON: And how is that coming along?

ORE: We're, um. / Going tomorrow…

NON: We're?

ORE: Him and me.

NON: He and I.

ORE: He and I. He's the one who told me to avenge you. He believes I can do it. He thinks I'm strong.

NON: I like the way he thinks.

ORE: Me too.

(NON *stares at them. He walks to the* YOUNG WOMAN, *crouches to pick her up off of the floor, stops.*)

NON: She doesn't have a name. Neither do I, now.

ORE: I want to honor you. I want to do something for you, in your name. I want to make you proud.

(NON *goes to the bed, tucks them in.*)

NON: Then do it.

Scene Nine

(*The backyard. Early, early morning*)

(ELLE *stands in the yard, over* BUDDY COX's *lifeless body, with an axe. She's struggling to chop off one of his limbs.*)

(CLYT *enters from the house, stands at a distance, watches.*)

CLYT: Elle?

(…)

ELLE: *(Not turning)* What.

CLYT: What happened to your bathing suit?

ELLE: I cut it.

CLYT: Is that Mister Cox?

ELLE: Yes.

CLYT: Did he harm you? *(…)* I could've done it.

ELLE: I did it myself.

CLYT: I could've helped.

ELLE: I didn't need any help! *(She swings the axe ineffectually.)*

CLYT: Do you want me to do this?

ELLE: No.

CLYT: There's a trick to it. I can show you.

ELLE: Please. Just leave me alone.

CLYT: All right.

(Thunder in the distance)

CLYT: Shovels are in the garage.

ELLE: Okay.

CLYT: Do you have bags?

ELLE: I'll get them.

CLYT: They're under the kitchen sink.

ELLE: Okay.

CLYT: I found double-bagging to be worth the effort. *(She turns to go.)* I don't know where you are planning to bury him, but you are standing over your father and Candy, so this part of the yard is spoken for. I imagine there's room over by the azaleas.

ELLE: Thanks.

CLYT: I'll just be inside. Don't stay out too late, dear.

(ELLE *continues to chop at the body.* CLYT *stands by the house, watches.*)

Scene Ten

(*The backyard. Early evening. Music plays.*)

(ETHEL *and* RHODA *stand at the table, on which a lit birthday cake sits.* ETHEL *is videotaping with a flip cam.* ELLE *sits on a pool chair, watching.*)

(THUS *leads* CLYT *out of the house with his hands over her eyes.*)

THUS: Watch your step!

CLYT: Where are you taking me, you naughty boy?

THUS: Just a little bit further.

CLYT: Are we outside? Mm. I smell the pool. I smell the grass. I also smell bourbon. Is Rhoda here?

(THUS *removes his hands from* CLYT's *eyes.*)

ETHEL, RHODA, THUS: SURPRISE!

CLYT: Oh my goodness!
What a surprise!
Oh, no, you
shouldn't have!
Oh, you can't!

(ETHEL, RHODA *and* THUS *sing a birthday song.*)

CLYT: How sweet of you all! And Elle! Thank you for being here.

ETHEL: Blow out your candles!

CLYT: Oh, no, it'd start a brush fire from all the heat! (*She blows out her candles.*) Champagne all around! Give a glass to my daughter, too. Tonight our ages don't matter! *(She raises her glass.)* A toast.

(ETHEL, RHODA and THUS raise glasses.)

CLYT: To dear friends. To children.

(ELLE downs the contents of her glass.)

CLYT: To lovers.

ETHEL: To newfound fame!

CLYT: Oh, Ethel, it's much too much but, yes: to the many new friends I've made, to the cyber sisters.

RHODA: To the sisters!

ETHEL: To you!

CLYT: All right: to me!

(They all drink.)

CLYT: Oh! And look at the fireflies! How they glow. Like little stars. It's as if we were having a party in the clouds. I feel like dancing.

(CLYT goes to THUS, dances with him. She kisses him.)

ETHEL: Ooooh!

RHODA: Aaaaaoooooo!

ETHEL: Get a room!

RHODA: Please don't!

CLYT: Oh, are you two feeling left out? There's enough of me to go around! *(She kisses ETHEL.)* It's my birthday! *(She kisses RHODA.)* Goodness, Rhoda, you're like a brewery.

(CLYT goes to ELLE and sneaks a quick kiss on her forehead. ELLE sits motionless.)

CLYT: I love this song. I love this night. Tonight feels fated, doesn't it?

ETHEL: I love birthdays!

RHODA: I love cake!

CLYT: I love this house.

ETHEL: I love the stars and the trees!

RHODA: I love warm summer air that feels like a hug!

CLYT: I love this dress.

THUS: I love doing the announcements at school!

ETHEL: I love rubbing my bare feet on a carpet!

RHODA: I love Debra Winger!

THUS: I love catching a fucking football!

CLYT: I love that oak tree and the tire swing.

ETHEL: I love N P R!

RHODA: I love gas tax holidays!

CLYT: I love sleeping with Thus' arms around me.

THUS: I love pooping!

ETHEL: I love peeing in the shower!

RHODA: I love a drink in the morning!

ETHEL: I love reading people's mail!

CLYT: I love life, I love my, I love…

(CLYT *stops. Covers her face, weeps. Everyone stops as well, watches her.*)

CLYT: (*Recovered*) Oh, let's celebrate! Let's all dance. Let's get crazy. Tonight let's be beautiful bodies dancing in the night, dancing in the clouds. Let the neighbors file a noise complaint. They're just jealous. Turn it up, Rhoda!

(They all dance, except for ELLE, who watches from her chair.

(LAD *and* ORE *emerge from the house. They are dressed nicely for the party.* ORE *carries a wrapped present.*)

(THUS *notices them first, stops dancing. Then* RHODA *and*
ETHEL. CLYT *continues to dance, unaware, or maybe aware,
until* ETHEL *goes and shuts off the music.*)

ORE: Oh, don't stop on account of us. Dance. You all
looked fuckin' fan-tastic.

(No one moves.)

ORE: This is Lad.

LAD: Hey. Nice to meet you.

ORE: Sorry we're late. *(To* LAD*)* Oh, we missed the
candles. *(Nodding to* ETHEL *and* RHODA*)* Mrs Whitman.
Mrs Sinclair. *(To* ELLE*)* Hey sis. *(…)* Happy Birthday,
Mom. *(He goes to her, kisses her on the cheek.)* Got you
something.

(ORE *hands* CLYT *the present. She stares at it.*)

ORE: It's just a little something, nothing fancy. Didn't
exactly get a severance package. Open it!

(CLYT *does. It's a copy of* A Thousand Splendid Suns.)

CLYT: Oh…thank you. This is very.

ORE: Ah, it's nothin'. *(To* THUS*)* Hey man.

THUS: Hey.

ORE: *(Extending a hand)* Didn't catch your name.

THUS: Thus.

ORE: Thus. I'm Ore. This is Lad.

THUS: Hey. Welcome home.

ORE: *(To* LAD*)* Did you hear that? He said welcome
home. *(To* THUS*)* Thanks, man. Sorry we don't have
anything for you.

THUS: That's okay. My birthday's in March.

ORE: Ah, fuck. We missed it. Well: belated?

(ORE withdraws a gun and shoots THUS, who crumples to the ground.)

RHODA:	ETHEL:
AAAAAAHHHHHH!!!	AAAAAAHHHHHH!!!

| LAD: Whoa. Whoa. You feel that? You feel that? | RHODA: Sweet Lord in / Ave Maria, hallowed be thy name! |

(LAD kisses ORE.)

| LAD: You did it, man. That was so good. I'm so fuckin' proud of you. I knew you could. You feel good? I feel good. | ETHEL: We're just here for a party! That's all, don't want any trouble! Just a party! |

RHODA: *(Lying down on the ground)* Do with us what you will! We / won't put up a fight! I'll bear Ethel's burden!

LAD: What? God. / No.

ETHEL: Rhoda, for goodness' sakes, get / up off of the ground.

LAD: C'mon, stop screaming already. Fuck. Cut it out.

ORE: *(To CLYT)* Stand up.

(She does.)

ORE: Don't look at me like that.

CLYT: Like what?

ORE: Don't look at me.

CLYT: All right. (...) Well.

ORE: Well.

CLYT: I suppose you had to do that.

ORE: Yup.

CLYT: He was just a boy.

ORE: Eh. Not so sure about that.

CLYT: He loved me, in his way.

ORE: He was no Dad.

CLYT: Actually, he was. Just young. *(Gesturing to* LAD*)* Does he make you happy?

LAD: I think your / son is…

*(*CLYT *holds up a hand and silences* LAD*.)*

CLYT: I asked my son.

ORE: Yeah.

CLYT: Good. *(She goes to the table, refills the champagne glasses.)* Let's toast to you.

*(*CLYT *passes out champagne glasses to everyone present.)*

CLYT: *(Raising her glass)* To my son Ore. Welcome home. And welcome to…

LAD: Lad.

CLYT: Lad. Welcome to Lad. My blessing to you both.

*(*LAD *takes* ORE*'s hand. They all drink.)*

LAD: *(To* ORE*)* You gonna do it?

ORE: *(Small)* Yeah.

CLYT: Anyone mind if I smoke? *(She pulls a pack of cigarettes out from under a pool chair.)* Secret stash. One last indulgence. Anyone?

LAD: Sure.

*(*CLYT *hands* LAD *a cigarette. He pulls a lighter from his pocket and lights both of their cigarettes.* RHODA *helps herself to more champagne.)*

CLYT: *(Enjoying the cigarette)* Guess these won't be the death of me. *(To* ORE*)* I knew you'd come. Tonight, I knew you'd come tonight. You were waiting.

ORE: I was.

CLYT: It was thoughtful of you. I'm moved, that you thought of me. *(To* LAD*)* Take care of my son. I'm sure you've noticed his looks.
Everything is steel cut, from his father, but he has my soft eyes and my hair, and. It won't last. The eyes will sink and the neck will soften, and forgive him that, as he should forgive you the same. *(She wipes her eyes.)* You're very kind to let me just have these few minutes. I'm, I am… *(Inhales)* …letting them wash over me. I am not angry with you for killing me, I understand, and quite frankly, this is the most attention that either of you have paid me your entire lives. It is rather beautiful, I think. I am looking at you. You are looking at me. You are mine in this moment. *(To* RHODA *and* ETHEL*)* Goodbye, girls. I shudder to think about what will become of our book club, but here.

(CLYT hands them A Thousand Splendid

Suns.)

CLYT: Put that on the list.

ETHEL: We will.

CLYT: Elle. I hope you continue to make movies, and / I hope that you never…

ELLE: *(Softly)* Oh my god. No, no, no.

CLYT: I know you wanted to be the one to do this, dear. But killing women is man's work.

ELLE: *(To* ORE*)* Come on, this is. Freaking me out.

LAD: Me too.

(…)

CLYT: *(To* ORE*)* I'm ready.

(ORE *raises his gun.)*

CLYT: I love you.

(...)

ORE: *(Suddenly crying)* It could be like this.

LAD: What?

ORE: Like this, just like this. We could forget it all, we could turn the music back on. You could hold my hand and Mom could bless us and Elle could film it and we could have a party.

ELLE: *(Crying as well)* Yes. Yes, oh my god, yes. Please, Mom? That sounds so nice.	LAD: What? No, that's not how it.
CLYT: No.	ORE: Yes, it could. It could be like this.
ELLE: Why not? This feels good. I want this. I need this. Mom?	LAD: This is what you came here to do.
CLYT: It cannot be. It cannot be.	ORE: I'm changing my mind! I can't do it!

ORE: *(He places his gun on the ground, kneels, crawls to* CLYT, *hugs her. Sobbing)* I don't want to!

CLYT: You have to.

ORE: No! Who says!

CLYT: I say.

ELLE: We don't care what you did! / Just be our mom!

CLYT: What are you doing?

ORE: I love you!

(CLYT *picks up his gun from the ground.)*

CLYT: This is not love. This / is weakness.

ELLE: Can we please have
a party? Can we
please just have a   ORE: Then I'm weak!
party?

LAD: No, man, no: I love you!
you're strong!

CLYT: I cannot live with my life, with what I've done,
and you show me no mercy. You will make me live
another day? Where is my son?

(CLYT *tries to hand* ORE *the gun. He swats it away.*)

ORE: No.

CLYT: Yes.

ORE: No.

CLYT: Do it!

ORE: No!

ELLE: Mom, please!

ORE: Mom, please!

CLYT: *(Scary)* HOW DARE YOU OFFER ME THIS
NOW! I KILLED YOUR FATHER! I drove an ax
through his body! I cut off the arms he'd throw you
baseballs with, the legs with which he chased after you
in the basement. I killed his whore, I cut her in twain.
You sniveling pansy FUCKING LITTLE GIRL—you
are nothing like your father. Your father was a big
dumb throbbing cock but he did what he wanted and
he didn't think twice. You came here to avenge him.
Act like him, for once! *(...)* No? Fine. I will.

(CLYT *raises the gun, shoots* LAD, *who falls down dead.*
ELLE *screams.* RHODA *and* ETHEL *cower.*)

ELLE: ORE?!

(ORE *swings around, cries out.*)

CLYT: How about now?

(CLYT *offers* ORE *the gun. He doesn't even notice. He lets go of her.*)

ORE: (*Small child*) What? (*He crawls to* LAD.) He's not breathing. What do I do?!

ELLE: I don't know! I don't know!!

ORE: (*Beginning C P R*)
One, two, three, four…   CLYT: He's dead.

Five, six, seven, eight…   ELLE: He's not dead!

Nine, ten, eleven,   CLYT: He's dead. I
twelve…   killed him.

ORE: Thirteen, fourteen, / fifteen…

CLYT: (*To* ORE) Why are you doing C P R? Haven't you seen this before?

ORE: (*Falling back*) He's dead.

CLYT: (*Raising her glass*) To the public school system.

ELLE: Oh my god.

ORE: He's dead. Why? Why is he dead?!

(ORE *weeps.* ELLE *tries to hold him, but he pushes her away, clutches* LAD's *hand, cries into the palm of it.*)

CLYT: I was hoping for a knee-jerk reaction.

ORE: He was mine!

CLYT: Exactly!

ORE: He loved me.

CLYT: Love is a myth.

ORE: Love is a god.

CLYT: A god!

ORE: Love is a god and I believe in him. Love is a god and I go to him. (*He brings the gun to his own forehead.*)

ELLE: No…no, no, no, no!

(ORE *shoots himself.* ELLE *screams. He falls, dead.*)

CLYT: Oh. Oh no. Oh no, / oh no, oh no.

ELLE: Look what you did!

CLYT: What I did?!

ELLE: Didn't you love us?

CLYT: You loved him more than me.

ELLE: Who, Dad? I wonder why! He didn't kill people!

CLYT: He killed my child! I was with child, I was with a third child, and he—he convinced me to, oh, to—as if he owned my body and could beckon children from it whenever he saw fit, make pessimists of my breasts, and I am sorry but after that I could not look at you.

(CLYT *collapses to the ground.* ETHEL *and* RHODA *rush to her, hold her.*)

CLYT: *(To* ELLE*)* Will you?

ELLE: Will I what?

CLYT: Kill me?

ELLE: I'm your child!

CLYT: Yes. Yes, you are only a child.

(ELLE *tosses herself on* ORE's *body, sobs.* CLYT *goes, wriggles the gun from* ORE's *hand.*)

CLYT: I am sorry. *(She turns to* RHODA *and* ETHEL.*)* Girls?

(CLYT *gestures for* RHODA *and* ETHEL *to join her. They begin to walk off with her.*)

CLYT: *(Turning back)* Well! I.

(CLYT *turns, leaves with them.* ELLE *rolls onto her back, having a coughing fit. She sits up, stumbles over to the table.*)

ELLE: Oh god, oh god, oh god. *(She drinks from the champagne bottle.)*

THUS: *(Stirring)* Uhhh…

ELLE: Thus?

(THUS tries to sit up, cries out in pain.)

THUS: FUCK!

(THUS gasps. ELLE kneels beside him.)

THUS: *(Choking)* Fuck. It hurts.

ELLE: You're dying.

THUS: Why?

ELLE: I don't know.

(There's a nearby gunshot.)

THUS: What was that?

ELLE: World's ending.

(THUS takes ELLE's hand.)

THUS:	OFFSTAGE WHISPERS:
I'm scared.	*LOLOLOLOLOLOLOL*
ELLE: Me too.	*LOLOLOLOLOLOLOL*

(ELLE puts the champagne bottle to THUS's lips. He drinks.)

THUS:	OFFSTAGE WHISPERS:
I'm so scared.	*LOLOLOLOLOLOLOL*

(ELLE leans in and kisses THUS.)

	OFFSTAGE WHISPERS:
	LOLOLOLOLOLOLOL

(THUS kisses ELLE back. He tries to touch her, but the pain is too great.)

THUS:	OFFSTAGE WHISPERS:
AGH!	*LOLOLOLOLOLOLOL*

ELLE: OFFSTAGE WHISPERS:
Ssshhh.   *LOLOLOLOLOLOLOL*

(ELLE *kisses* THUS *again.*)

                                       OFFSTAGE WHISPERS:
                                       LOLOLOLOLOLOLOL

(ELLE *sits on top of* THUS, *begins to gently have sex with him. Sirens are heard, drawing near.*)

THUS: OFFSTAGE WHISPERS:
Oww…   *LOLOLOLOL oh Elle*
                                       oh Elle

ELLE: OFFSTAGE WHISPERS:
Oww…   *Oh Elle Oh Elle Oh*
                                       Elle Oh Elle Oh Elle

(RHODA *and* ETHEL *enter,* CLYT's *body slung over* RHODA's *shoulder. They lower her onto the ground.* ETHEL *carries an axe and shovels. They look at the yard, count the bodies, and put their hands on their hips: they've got a lot of work to do. They begin to dig.*)

THUS: OFFSTAGE WHISPERS:
I don't want to die.   *OH ELLE OH ELLE OH*
                                       ELLE OH ELLE

ELLE: OFFSTAGE WHISPERS:
Me either.   *OH ELLE OH ELLE OH*
                                       ELLE OH ELLE

THUS: OFFSTAGE WHISPERS:
I don't want to die.   *OH ELLE OH ELLE OH*
                                       ELLE OH ELLE

ELLE: OFFSTAGE WHISPERS:
Me either.   OH ELLE OH ELLE OH
                                       ELLE OH ELLE OH
                                       ELLE OH ELLE OH
                                       ELLE OH ELLE OH

ELLE OH ELLE OH
ELLE OH ELLE

(Siren lights. Flashbulbs from cameras. Police radios.
Shovels digging. Fingers typing)

END OF PLAY

www.ingramcontent.com/pod-product-compliance
Lightning Source LLC
Chambersburg PA
CBHW052125090426
42741CB00009B/1961